ACCLAIM FOR AWARD WINNING AUTHOR BARRY FINLAY

THE GUARDIANS OF TRUTH
A JAKE SCOTT MYSTERY

"Perfectly executed, well written, thoroughly and utterly enjoyable; I really do hope Jake doesn't stop scratching that journalistic itch, because I'd love to spend another few hundred pages in his company."
—Cath 'N' Kindle Book Reviews

SEARCHING FOR TRUTH
A JAKE SCOTT MYSTERY

"Searching For Truth is an intriguing whodunit that embraces much more psychological depth than most mysteries and will have readers both guessing and involved to the end."—D. Donovan, Senior Reviewer, Midwest Book Review

THE BURDEN OF DARKNESS
A MARCIE KANE AND NATHAN HARRIS THRILLER

"Thoroughly captivating, ingenious, and full of heart-pounding suspense, this is an action thriller done right..."—The Prairies Book Review

NEVER SO ALONE
A NATHAN HARRIS THRILLER NOVELLA

"Brilliant. Would be an amazing film!"—Goodreads reader

REMOTE ACCESS
AN INTERNATIONAL POLITICAL THRILLER

"While grounded in reality, Remote Access is a must-read with a singular sense of escapism rare in a political thriller."—BestThrillers.com

A PERILOUS QUESTION
AN INTERNATIONAL THRILLER AND CRIME NOVEL

"Written with a compassionate, knowledgeable voice, the book is an excellent story of mystery and intrigue."—**RECOMMENDED by the US Review of Books**

THE VANISHING WIFE
AN ACTION-PACKED CRIME THRILLER

"The pace grabs hold. Whether the mild-mannered accountant Mason Seaforth could actually pull off what's at stake depends on the colour, the energy and dialogue of the story telling. The Vanishing Wife is convincing."—**Donald Graves, Canadian Crime Reviews**

KILIMANJARO AND BEYOND A LIFE-CHANGING JOURNEY

"The book reads like a journal and the writing is warm, familiar and humorous. 'Kilimanjaro and Beyond, A Life-Changing Journey,' will challenge all who read it to consider how they too can make a difference, not only for others, but for themselves as well."—**Reader Views**

I GUESS WE MISSED THE BOAT
A TRAVEL MEMOIR

"This is an exhilarating read."—**Grady Harp, Amazon Hall of Fame reviewer**

JUST KEEP CLIMBING
INSPIRATIONAL STORIES FOR OVERCOMING CHALLENGES AND LIVING LIFE

"Bottom line, 'Just Keep Climbing' is an amazing source of inspiration and empowerment. It reminds us that when things get tough, we can still achieve our dreams."—**NorkDorf Entertainment**

THE SECRET TRUTH

A JAKE SCOTT MYSTERY

BARRY FINLAY

Published by Keep On Climbing Publishing

Copyright ©Barry Finlay 2024
(613) 240-6953
info@barry-finlay.com
www.barry-finlay.com

No part of this book may be reproduced, stored in a retrieval system, or transmitted in any form or by any means without the prior written permission of the publisher or, in case of photocopying or other reprographic copying, a license from Access Copyright (The Canadian Licensing Agency) 320-56 Wellesley Street West, Toronto, Ontario, M5S 2S3

Cataloguing data available at Library and Archives Canada.

ISBN: 978-1-0688371-0-4 Paperback
ISBN: 978-1-0688371-1-1 eBook

This book is a work of fiction. Names, characters, places and incidents are products of the author's imagination or are used fictitiously. Any resemblance to actual events or locales or persons, living or dead, is entirely coincidental.

ACKNOWLEDGEMENTS

IT'S ALWAYS ENJOYABLE to place Jake Scott in difficult situations, and *The Secret Truth* was no different. While Jake isn't the most modern guy you might come across, he thinks things through and usually comes up with a solution. He sometimes wishes things were the way they were in the "old days," but luckily, he's surrounded by people trying to drag him into the current century. Overall, it's my pleasure to work with the fictitious Jake.

As usual, there are several people to thank for helping me bring *The Secret Truth* to you, dear reader. And you are the ones I want to thank first this time. It's your positive feedback through book signings, messages, reviews, and comments on social media that encourages me to keep writing. It's knowing that people are waiting to find out what Jake is up to next that makes all this worthwhile. I spend a lot of time in my office banging away on the keyboard to create a story, and it's always so satisfying when positive comments come back.

Mirna Gilman from Books Go Social has designed each of the Jake Scott covers and she was once again responsible for this gem. I know when I give my concepts to Mirna, she will bring them to life. Thank you, Mirna. Sigrid Macdonald edited this book and made it better. I'm always amazed at what editors discover when I hand over a manuscript, but I've sort of come to expect it. Many thanks to Sigrid for her editing expertise. Indie Publishing Group formatted the manuscript to make it look like the final product you are reading now, so a hearty thanks goes to them.

The biggest thanks go to my wife, Evelyn, who reads and critiques the manuscript before anyone else sees it. Evelyn wears many hats when it comes to my writing: avid reader, promoter, critic, cheerleader, promoter… Oh, and did I mention promoter? She is my biggest fan and I'm deeply grateful.

Finally, I urge everyone to keep reading and supporting indie authors. Many books by indie authors are every bit as good as the well-known ones you will see at the front of the bookstore, so I urge you to support them. They deserve to be heard.

CHAPTER ONE

IN JUST A matter of hours, chaos would break loose.

Jake Scott's day started under control, albeit differently from the usual routine. He had awakened for the third of five days in a Bed and Breakfast apartment in an area called Westboro in Ottawa. The community Jake had called home his entire life lay on the west side of downtown, in Canada's capital.

Construction on the hardwood floors at his home precipitated his stay at the B&B. The owners listed the apartment as a self-contained, modern one-bedroom with Netflix in a house they called Sweet Dreams. Cleanliness and a private bathroom mattered to Jake, and the apartment fit the bill. He hadn't stayed in a room anywhere but at his home for a long time, so he had enjoyed talking to four other renters and the owners over the morning meal. Well, three of the renters. The other wasn't overly friendly.

Jake planned to spend the day killing time. After breakfast, he returned to his rented apartment, opened the drapes, and read an Agatha Christie novel. He stopped at the end of a chapter and examined his surroundings. The room featured a four-poster bed, floral wallpaper, one comfortable wingback armchair that Jake occupied, and an antique white nightstand. A decorative white bowl and pitcher with a rose emblazoned on the side sat on a round crocheted doily on the nightstand. While the bowl and pitcher appeared to be vintage, Jake suspected someone had made them in a ceramic class. A blue rectangular woven rug with a medallion pattern in the middle covered the center of the dark hardwood floor. It looked expensive. He saw a similar rug through the open door of one of the unused rooms down the hall and an identical but larger one in the dining room. Maybe the owners took advantage of a volume discount, he thought.

He remembered an article about rugs written by a colleague at the newspaper office where he used to work. From his recollection, it was a great article describing countries known for their rug-making. He seemed to recall Iran and Turkey, among others. He mulled over the fact that Turkey had changed its name to Türkiye somewhere along the way, but it had been Turkey his entire life.

The vintage motif in his room didn't carry over to the modern ensuite, which featured a shower with a glass enclosure and spray nozzles from top to bottom. It was like walking from the early 1900s into the future with a few steps. Even though he was by himself, Jake wasn't sure about the lack of privacy offered by the clear glass enclosure shower. Another nod to a crumbling civilization, he thought.

After reading a few pages, Jake's eyes blurred, and his head lolled on his neck. He snapped awake with a start when his neck muscles stretched and creaked as his head fell forward again. He gave up and allowed himself to doze off with his chin resting on his hand. When he woke an hour later, he walked to Brew and Buns, his favorite restaurant on Wellington Street, where he enjoyed a leisurely lunch.

The day continued to unfold routinely. He had left his temperamental cat, Oliver, at his friend Daniella Perez's condo, so he paid the feline a visit. Jake confirmed with Dani, as her friends called her, that her teenage daughter, Emilie, was home so the cat would enjoy her attention.

The seventeen-year-old greeted Jake at the door. She wore a broad smile and a trendy pale yellow top that stopped above her midriff, faded blue jeans, and bare feet. She padded across the room and flopped into an upholstered chair while folding her legs underneath her in one fluid motion.

Jake marveled at the flexibility of youth.

"How has he been?" he asked as he nodded toward Oliver, who approached from the hallway.

"He's been great. No problem. He's just looking for hugs."

Oliver confirmed the sentiment as he leaped onto Emily's lap and acknowledged Jake's presence with a sleepy glance.

Jake killed more time chatting with Emilie before dropping by his house to check the floors, which looked fabulous. He grabbed a sandwich at Brew and Buns before heading off to a pickleball game with new friends. In his never-ending quest to shed a few pounds, pickleball seemed like an enjoyable way to accomplish his goal while meeting new people. Some members of the group loved to win, while others just enjoyed the outing, but they all sat around a table relishing beer and chicken wings after the game. Jake suspected the post-game activity might defeat the purpose of losing weight, but he enjoyed it, nonetheless.

He had left his car parked in the driveway at his house, as everything he planned to do that day was within easy walking distance. Now, he savored a gorgeous June night as he sauntered back to the B&B from the pickleball courts around eleven o'clock. No bugs. Warm air, but not muggy. His shadow, cast by the streetlights lining the other side of the street, tagged along to his right, lagging behind but tracking his every step. The leaves whispered in the gentle breeze. Even with the glare of the streetlights, a planet he couldn't identify glowed like a brilliant marble in the night sky. The street remained quiet, spooky, as if aliens had swooped down from the shiny marble planet and made off with the local inhabitants. Occasional signs offered proof that life might still exist. A Toyota parked in the driveway here, an imposing black Ford F-150 over there, matching white Audis in a third. The dim glow of a table lamp filtered through one curtained window while the telltale blue light of a TV set glimmered through another. A flame flickered for an instant at a house across the street, followed by the glowing embers of a cigarette, which a man carried to the yawning doorway of his open garage. It all confirmed life still occupied the planet.

The only noises other than the whispering leaves were the sound of his gym bag slapping against his thigh with every step and his labored breathing. As if the pounding in his chest and the rivers of sweat he produced at the pickleball game weren't enough, the slight incline toward the intersecting street that beckoned in the near distance reminded Jake how out of shape he was. The post-pickleball game stiffness would arrive in the morning. He thought he should have taken the car, but his apartment lay only two blocks away now. He could crawl the remaining distance if he had to.

The sound of a car engine starting in the distance interrupted the calm of the night. Warm rubber on pavement chirped as the car pulled away. A dog barked at the sudden sound. Oblivious to the revving engine, Jake jaywalked to the other side of the street about halfway down the block at exactly the time the car careened around the corner. The headlights bounced off the corner house and veered in Jake's direction. A giant spotlight might as well have turned on him. For a split second, Jake stopped in mid-stride, staring wide-eyed and open-mouthed as the two brilliant headlights bore down on him at lightning speed.

Only instinct saved him. He leaped for the grassy area bordering the street as the car roared past, its engine screaming. Jake swore the driver's front corner bumper grazed the heel of his shoe an instant before his body thudded on the unforgiving ground. First, his knees, followed by his arms, and then his face completed the maneuver. The gym bag he launched during his dive landed with a dull smack on the sidewalk.

Jake turned his head to watch the car from his prone position, but all he could tell as the vehicle raced around the corner at the end of the block was that it was big and dark. For a second, streetlights glinted off the wheel disks and reflected off the passenger side windows. Then it disappeared. He moaned and, without moving his extended arm, raised his middle finger in the general direction of the car's path. While the car and its driver had vanished, the gesture gave him a measure of satisfaction.

He pulled himself upright, and, as everyone does at a time like that, Jake glanced up and down the street to see if anyone had observed his clumsy headfirst dive into the grass. Even the smoker had disappeared from the garage doorway. Jake spit gritty dirt from his mouth, wiped his face, and dusted the turf from his bare knees. His body quivered from the sudden shock of what had just happened. Blood tricked down his leg from a scrape on his kneecap, and his chin throbbed. When he dabbed at the pulsating spot on his face, the streetlight overhead reflected blood on his fingertips. He retrieved his gym bag from the sidewalk, unzipped the compartment, and removed a towel to dab at the wounds before zipping up the fabric duffle and hoisting it over his shoulder.

The quivering subsided, and, deciding everything still worked, although a little stiffer, Jake continued toward the B&B. He stumbled on numb feet with his first steps, but the sensation soon disappeared.

Once the full sensation returned to his feet, Jake continued to hobble down the street on his throbbing knee, but his troublesome night had not ended. The second he rounded the corner onto the street toward his temporary residence, the building housing the Bed and Breakfast erupted into a fireball of flames and flying debris.

CHAPTER TWO

GROUND TREMBLED UNDER Jake's feet, and streetlights and trees rocked as if a sudden fierce wind grabbed them by the throat and shook. The entire street shimmied for interminable seconds, and the pavement seemed to heave toward the heavens as if from an earthquake before settling back to earth. The sound of the blast echoed off the surrounding houses, and a car siren bleated nonstop. Jake's muscles wound themselves into knots for the second time in minutes. Goosebumps popped on his arms and the back of his neck, and his stomach twisted. Once again, his gym bag thudded to the ground from his unclenched fist as fiery roofing materials rained down onto the street and the cars in the B&B's driveway. As Jake's mouth hung open, a tree in front of the house burst into flames.

For the second time, instinct took over. People lived in that house! Jake shook himself from the shock gripping his body and leaned forward to rummage through his gym bag for his phone. He unzipped one end of his bag but located only his running shoes. He tossed the now bloody towel into the bag and fumbled with the zipper at the other end, hands shaking until he brushed against what he looked for. His heart sank when he held his phone in the brightness of the overhead streetlight to reveal a jagged crack snaking across the length of the screen. It must have cracked when the bag flew out of his hands during his earlier dive for safety. He recognized a man running past as the smoker from the garage.

Jake left the bag in a heap on the sidewalk and limped behind the smoker toward the burning house, jabbing at the numbers on his phone's keypad with his index finger as he went. At least it still worked as a 911 dispatcher answered and informed him someone had already called in the explosion. Sirens in the distance confirmed it. He hoped he might save the people inside, but his trembling, scratched legs and ragged breathing slowed his progress. When he arrived in front of the scene, the flames reflected off the anxious faces of the neighbors who gathered across the street, some of whom wore pajamas or housecoats over their night attire. One man wore only his jockey shorts. A woman held a towel over a cut, while blood streamed down her dazed face. Jake scanned the crowd as he leaned forward, gasping for breath with his hands on his knees, but saw none of the people he chatted with that morning. Two young men ran toward the house but shielded their faces with their arms as intense heat drove them back.

This can't be happening!

The scene was one of complete and utter devastation. Bricks and smoldering materials lay on the street as flames from the building lit the night sky. Jake thought a shriek came from inside the remnants of the building, but the sirens and screeching tires of the fire engines drowned out the sound. *Was it his imagination?* He couldn't be certain. He stared at the area where the B&B sat. His eyes saw the pile of rubble, but his brain refused to accept the message. As his mind came to grips with the impact of the scene, he realized nobody could have survived. Roaring flames licking from the windows and smoke curling from the remains of the house spoke of what happened. It would soon look like a bulldozer came onto the property, knocked everything down, and left a pile of burning construction material behind. The shriek he thought he heard had to be his imagination or something related to the fire engines and police cars arriving.

The building was a renovated three-story brick structure converted to a Bed and Breakfast by the owners. Smaller than some, Jake considered it to be comfortable enough. Now that he paid attention to the houses on either side, he realized that builders had constructed them of bricks similar to the Bed and Breakfast. Each of the three houses featured large yards by city standards. The rooftops of the neighboring houses immediately right and left of the devastated building also burned. The explosion had caved in the side of the house on the left as if a giant wrecking ball struck it. Windows in both houses had disappeared, or the glass had been spider-webbed from the blast. A large, ragged hole in the windshield belonging to the vehicle in the righthand driveway suggested that a brick might have sailed through it. The cars parked in the B&B driveway lay under piles of smoldering debris. They parked two-by-two and end to end, but it was difficult to tell where one ended and another started now. Smoldering branches from the burning tree lay on top of the mess.

Jake scanned the street on both sides to see several houses had been affected. The explosion had lifted roofs and crumpled garage doors. Looking over his shoulder, he noticed damaged windows in houses across the street from the B&B. People still emerged from homes, some wide-eyed and confused.

The true impact of the devastation slowly sank in for Jake. Two police officers, who had somehow arrived without him noticing, pushed the crowd back. Jake heard the officer who appeared to be in charge mention "gas" to two other cops while telling them to "control the onlookers." Many in the crowd held up phones, hoping to capture lightning in a bottle for a viral social media video.

Jake hadn't smelled the odor before, but now the police officer mentioned it, he could almost taste it. He didn't know if it was gas or propane. A mixture of fumes and acrid smoke hung in the air. The officers pushed the gathering farther down the street more brusquely now, their determined faces suggesting concern that gas migration could cause additional explosions. Other police officers established a perimeter with yellow tape in front of the Bed and Breakfast and houses across and down the street. Jake thought there had to be at least twelve houses that people wouldn't return to tonight.

A firefighter rushed to the front of the group. He stalked up and down in front of the gathering, making eye contact and shouting, "Does anyone know anything about that house? How many people lived there?"

Unintelligible murmuring rose from the crowd. One man shouted, "I suspect they used it for short-term rentals."

The firefighter nodded as if he already knew that and repeated his question. "Do you know how many were in the building? Anybody else know *anything*?" He gestured with his arms at the crowd. "Come on, hurry. We need answers, and fast!"

Jake realized he might help, so he pushed his way to the front of the crowd and caught the firefighter's attention.

"I stayed there. I was walking back from a pickleball game when I saw the explosion. At least six people besides me were in the house this morning. The owner and his wife, a couple, a young woman, and another man."

Some in the crowd within hearing distance gasped at Jake's count. A utility truck slid to a stop among the gathered vehicles, and as the driver hurriedly approached, the firefighter turned to him to explain that it could have been a gas explosion. At the firefighter's urging, the truck's two occupants hustled off to shut off the main valve.

Jake's phone vibrated in his pocket, but before he had time to check it, the firefighter turned back to him. "Okay, so you say six or more people were in the house?"

"This morning, yes, but I don't know who checked in or out today. I was out all day."

The firefighter locked eyes with Jake for a few seconds, processing the information. He turned on his heel and ran toward the front of the trucks, where men and women in yellow helmets and black and yellow coats with reflective stripes aimed a mix of chemicals and water at the burning structures. The firefighter who questioned Jake gestured down the street and around the corner. Two firefighters ran in the direction he pointed. Presumably, Jake assumed, hoping to gain access to the back of the house to save anyone who might be alive inside. Others pounded on the doors of neighboring houses.

Jake's phone vibrated persistently in his pocket, but he remembered he should tell someone about the car that had nearly hit him. There might be some connection to the blast. He leaned over the police tape to shout and wave at an officer, who referred to the onlookers as lookie-loos as he moved them back. The police officer turned in his direction. Jake shouted above the din. The murmuring crowd, firefighters yelling instructions, crackling flames, idling engines, and pumping water hoses all contributed to the chaotic scene. An SUV with a local news decal on the door showed up, and a reporter and cameraman rushed toward the crowd, hoping they were the first on the scene.

"I need to talk to you," Jake said. "It could relate to the explosion."

The police officer regarded Jake as he hustled toward him. The arsonists on TV who return to the scene to admire their handiwork flashed through Jake's mind, and it occurred to him that the police officer might imagine the same about him. Jake's phone vibrated again.

The burly police officer hoisted his pants. "Can I help you, sir?"

"I was staying at the B&B. As I returned this evening, a car almost ran me down on the street around the corner minutes before the explosion. It could be nothing, but I thought you should know."

The constable's face didn't change. He lifted the tape and gestured toward a marked police car parked at an angle behind the firetrucks.

"Follow me, please. I want to take a statement."

Jake did as he was told and followed the officer. Meanwhile, his pocket kept vibrating. When they arrived at the car, the officer opened the door so Jake could climb into the back seat while he got into the driver's side. The officer took out his phone and hit the record key. He asked Jake to state his name, why he stayed at the B&B, and why he was away from the house that night.

Jake explained he was a retired reporter, the construction work on his house, the name of the construction company, who he played pickleball with that night, and what he remembered about the people he met at breakfast. He knew an investigator would verify everything he said, so he tried to be as complete with his descriptions as possible. He realized the combined shock of almost being run over by the car and the explosion could prevent him from recalling everything clearly.

Jake continued to ignore the persistent buzzing of his phone. He had a pretty good idea who was calling.

The police officer said, "You mentioned that a car came close to hitting you on the way back to the B&B before the explosion?"

"Yes, I can't tell you much, other than the car was big and a dark color. It came around the corner fast and missed me by inches as I crossed the street."

"What time would that have been?"

"Shortly after eleven. The thing I wanted to tell you is that the car incident happened immediately before the blast. After I gathered myself together, which took a few minutes, I continued down the street. As soon as I turned the corner, the explosion happened."

"Did you see the license plate number or any part of it?"

"No, everything happened too fast. By the time I looked up, the car had driven around the next corner."

"Did you see where the car came from?"

"Other than from the street where the explosion occurred, no."

"Are you sure they parked on that street?"

"Only judging from when the car started to when it turned the corner onto the street I walked on. The neighborhood was quiet, so I heard the car start. It was a few seconds…less than a minute. I suppose it could have come from a side street. It was moving."

The constable looked at his phone. Jake assumed he wanted to make sure it was still recording.

"Are you certain it was the car that nearly hit you that you heard starting?"

Jake realized it could have been any car he heard and that this one may have come from anywhere. "No, I can't be certain."

"Okay, thank you for bringing this to my attention. I'm going to assign a case number, and I'd like you to go to the station tomorrow.

Give them the number, and someone will ask you the same questions to see if you remember anything more. They'll ask you to diagram where you were on the street relative to the car. In the meantime, please call the station if anything else comes to mind and don't leave town."

At this point, people in TV crime shows would ask indignantly, "Why? Am I a suspect?" But Jake knew that until the investigators confirmed his claims of his whereabouts, it seemed suspicious that he was away from the B&B when it blew up. The officer asked if Jake wanted to enter the case number on his phone, but remembering the cracked screen, he declined. The officer climbed out of the car, opened the back door for Jake, and handed him a piece of paper with the case number. After tucking the paper into his wallet, Jake finally looked at his phone. A string of texts and three phone messages greeted him.

The texts were short and to the point and became increasingly urgent.

I heard about the explosion. Are you okay?
Where are you? Call me when you get this message.
I need to know you're okay. Call me.
Call me!

They all came from the phone of a homicide detective with the Ottawa Police Service and his friend Daniella Perez.

CHAPTER THREE

THE HARDWOOD FLOORS at Jake's home had shown clear signs of wear. Once shiny, the floors looked dull in high-traffic areas. The inconsistent coloring and scratches demanded refinishing. He put off the work for years. He and his late wife, Mia, had even talked about refinishing the floors before she died, but it never happened. Finally, as the scratches became more noticeable by the day when the sun was shining through the sunroom window, Jake pulled the trigger with a contractor, and the floors would be shiny and new once again. In the meantime, the work forced Jake to vacate because the refinished floor would emit toxic fumes for the first few days. The contractor suggested he stay away for three to five days. Jake, the ever practical one, chose five.

He could have stayed with his friend, Daniella, but she had a visitor, a former colleague from out of town. Dani, as her friends called her, was a Venezuelan beauty Jake had met two years ago. She and Jake were working on a personal relationship, but they each had baggage they needed to get past. Jake had lost his wife, Mia, to an aneurysm, and Dani had gone through a nasty divorce. They agreed to take their relationship day by day to see where it would go.

While Dani said she could ask her visitor to stay in a hotel, Jake would hear none of it and insisted on finding accommodation elsewhere. Dani surprised Jake when she offered to take his cat, Oliver, for the week. She never seemed to like the cat and questioned why Jake put up with Oliver's temperamental disposition. Jake always thought she saw the cat at his worst. Not surprising since Oliver acted that way most of the time.

Jake wandered down the street, far enough from the commotion that he would be able to hear, and dialed Dani's number. Dani was always professional at work, and her job introduced her to the worst of humanity, but a panicked voice greeted Jake from the other end of the line.

"I'm so glad to hear your voice. Are you okay? The news about the explosion came over the radio when they dispatched the officers. I knew you were staying at that B&B. You told me you were playing pickleball, but why didn't you call me sooner? I've been worried sick."

"I'm fine. The B&B blew up when I turned the corner to the street it's on, but I wasn't hurt. There had to be people still inside, though. I didn't see any of the people I ate breakfast with on the street. A car nearly ran me down just before the explosion, so I explained all that to an officer here. That's why I couldn't call sooner. I hope your night has been quieter."

Silence hung in the air for a few seconds as Jake assumed Dani's detective mind connected the car that almost ran him down with the blast. He understood from experience she would analyze the information he gave her before asking questions. He also knew her Hispanic traits from being born in Venezuela could be explosive, and he might still be on blast for not calling her sooner. She seemed to take the high road, at least for the time being.

"You've had quite the night. I'm relieved you're okay." Her voice calmed as she described her night. "There was another stabbing outside a bar in the Byward Market, so that's where I've been. At least it doesn't appear to be random. According to witnesses, two men got into a confrontation over a girl, and one came back with a knife. You know the rest of the story. A fight ensued in the alley, and one stabbed the other multiple times. He disappeared into the night, but witnesses gave us detailed descriptions of the man the victim argued with." A mirthless chuckle followed. "So far, he's described as looking like everyone from Brad Pitt to Shrek, but we'll get him. What's this about a car nearly running you down?"

Jake knew the Byward Market area to be Ottawa's entertainment district, with many bars, restaurants, and shopping venues. But there it was. Dani zeroed in on the speeding car. For the second time, Jake explained about the reckless driver. He felt foolish when he said, "I didn't get a description other than the car was big and a dark color. I wish I looked up sooner to see the license plate, but I was flat on my face. I felt better when I flipped the driver off, even though he or she turned the corner by that time."

Dani chuckled. "I understand. It would have made me feel better for sure if I were in your shoes. Don't worry about the license. It sounds like everything happened fast. The speeding car and the explosion could be coincidence, although I'm not a big believer in those, as you know. I'm sure the investigators will check security and traffic cameras in the area to trace the car's route and try to identify the driver. They'll also ask anyone with information to come forward. In the meantime, my team and I need to focus on the stabbing downtown. I'm just glad you're still around to talk about it after your double whammy tonight. What did the officer tell you to do?"

"They want me to go to the station tomorrow to describe the people staying at the B&B, draw a sketch of the car's route as much as I know it, and give them any other information that I recall between now and then. I must admit, I'm still a little shaken."

Dani hesitated for a few beats before responding. She surprised Jake when she did.

"Do me a favor and find something to do until the afternoon. Drop in to see me when you're done with the officer at the station."

"Uh, okay. That won't be hard. I'm meeting the guys for breakfast tomorrow morning. Any reason you want me to wait until the afternoon?"

"Gosh, is tomorrow Saturday already? Where does the time go? I want to see you to confirm you're okay, but I might ask you to do something for me. It'll have to be hush-hush."

Jake waited for Dani to elaborate, but she said nothing more. Instead, she said, "Speaking of sleeping, where are you going to sleep tonight?"

The question caught Jake off guard.

"I didn't even think of that, but you're right, I can't go home yet. The floors looked amazing this afternoon, but I still smelled the chemicals. I'll drop into the house to pick up some clothes and rent a motel room. I'll only be out of the house two more nights."

"Here's an idea," Dani said. "How about Emilie sleeps on an air mattress in my room? I'll give her room to my friend, and you can sleep on the couch. It will be nice and cozy and work out for everyone. Don't say 'no,'" she added as if the decision were final. "You can visit Oliver."

It was Jake's turn to chuckle. "I visited Oliver this afternoon, and I don't expect he realized I was there. Nor did he care. He's more Emilie's cat than mine. Thanks, Dani. I appreciate your offer, I do, but I can't put everyone out like that. I've slept on air mattresses before, and they never hold air all night. It's not fair to Emilie either."

After going back and forth a few times, the rarest thing happened. Jake won an argument with Dani, although sleeping on a motel bed may not qualify as a win. After a grumpy request from Dani to call her the next day, they hung up.

Jake wandered back toward the scene, but the police had cordoned off more of the street, so he couldn't get anywhere near where he stood earlier. He and other bystanders watched the firefighters continue to subdue the fire, which now seemed under control. They had quelled the flames on the neighboring houses and reduced the B&B to a smoldering mess. His stomach sank when he peered through the smoke to see paramedics waiting with stretchers on gurneys on the street in front of the house. He hoped they were at the scene to rescue someone, but by this time, it would more likely be a recovery. Then he spotted two paramedics leaning over a body on the ground. One held an oxygen mask to the person's face while the other feverishly pumped on the victim's chest. Their frantic actions didn't look good. An officer cleared debris from the cars in the driveway and appeared to be taking photos of license plate numbers. It would be a way of narrowing down the identification process of those inside.

Jake walked to his house and unlocked the door. Holding his breath as long as he could, he entered and filled his gym bag with an assortment of casual clothes. He grabbed the laptop he had left behind when he moved out. Thinking it would be nice to be away from the computer for five days, he had made the fortuitous decision to leave it at the house. Now he realized he could have been buying a new laptop along with the razor and other toiletries he needed to replace the ones buried under a pile of rubble.

He locked the door again and retrieved his Subaru Outback, which he drove past McDonald's and the Civic Hospital on Carling Avenue, to a hotel north and west of his community. When the exhausted-looking female clerk nudged her glasses up her nose with her index finger and regarded him oddly, he realized he must appear like a street bum with his scraped knee, the raspberry-colored scratch on his chin, and his disheveled clothing. He probably stank of smoke and other fumes from the fire, too. All he needed was a bottle in a brown paper bag to complete the image. She had undoubtedly seen worse as she coded two plastic keys and tucked them inside a paper envelope while pointing out the Wi-Fi passcode scrawled on the envelope.

He took the elevator and limped down the hall's well-worn carpet. A mild disinfectant odor hung in the air when he opened the door to the second-floor room and flicked on the hall light. It was a standard room with a 45-inch TV hanging from a bracket on the wall, a wooden desk with a lamp and outlets to charge a phone and plug in a laptop, one chair, and a king-sized bed that sagged in the middle. A small chuckle escaped his lips at the sight of the bed. It took up most of the room and made his queen bed at home look like a single. Most importantly, a kettle, cups, and the fixings necessary for coffee sat at one end of the desk with a mini bar at the other end.

Jake tossed his gym bag onto the nylon straps of a folding luggage rack beside the mini bar and adjusted the thermostat to slow the cold air blasting into the room. He kept his jacket on until the room warmed a little. The clock on the bedside table displayed 12:53 a.m. Too late for the news on TV, so he switched on the radio and the lamp beside the bed. He tapped the volume control repeatedly to turn it down when a rock song he didn't recognize blared from the radio's speaker.

He glanced through the dirty window to a parking lot with a variety of cars filling the white-lined spaces. Lightning split the sky to the west. Most of the windows in the U-shaped building were dark, although lights snaked around the drapes in a room on the third floor across the parking lot from his and another on the second. He pulled the sheer drapes together. They seemed dusty, like housekeeping had neglected to wipe them down recently, so he wiped his hand on his shorts. A TV show he saw a few years back about the cleanliness, or lack thereof, of hotel rooms left him paranoid.

He shut out the outside world by pulling the rods of the thick, blue blackout drapes together. He plugged his phone into the outlet on the desk, and too tired to shower, he washed his face and hands. The dried blood on his knee and chin came off with a gentle dabbing of a wet facecloth, and scabs had already started forming. He forgot to pack a disinfectant and band-aids before he left the house, so he jotted a reminder on a notepad to pick some up in the morning along with other essentials. He shut off the hall light. Still cold, he pulled off his running shoes, and lay fully clothed and shivering under the comforter on the bed with his arms crossed. Out of a longstanding habit, he never pulled hotel blankets high enough to touch his face.

The explosion headlined the local radio news at 1:00 a.m. A female reporter at the scene spoke excitedly about the blast. Jake thought he recognized the voice of the man being interviewed as the officer he spoke to. His name was Constable Bill Leeds, and he said the cause of the fire was still under investigation, but there was no reason to believe the explosion resulted from foul play. He said he couldn't speculate any further, but then he did when he added it was likely a gas or propane explosion. When asked about the people inside, he said, "I can confirm at least one fatality. We believe others are missing. We will hold a press conference tomorrow when we have more information."

Jake's stomach flipped at the mention of a fatality, although it didn't surprise him. He frowned when the officer mentioned they didn't suspect foul play. The speeding car popped into his head. He reached over to shut off the radio and resumed his position with his arms across his chest. The mini bar tempted him, but his knee hurt, and the rest of his body ached like a rather large truck had run him over. Every time he flexed his jaw muscles, the skin around the scrape on his chin tightened to remind him it would require attention in the morning. It seemed like too much effort to get up. He turned off the bedside lamp, plunging the room into darkness, except for a red light blinking from the smoke detector on the wall near the ceiling and the reflection from the illuminated numbers on the clock.

Sleep eluded him as a kaleidoscope of thoughts tumbled through his mind. First, the speeding car. Then, the explosion. The fatalities and their families. Dani. Emilie. Oliver. Turning on his side, away from the blinking red light, he tried to focus on one thing. Anything but the car or the explosion and the resulting fatality. His relationship with Dani always pleased him, although the complications of their personal baggage seemed to get in the way. He settled on focusing on the shiny new floors in his house and drifted off to sleep.

CHAPTER FOUR

JAKE WOKE TO the sound of wind and rain slashing against the window. The darkness disoriented him for a few seconds, but when he noticed the blinking light on the smoke detector, he remembered he was in a hotel room. Memories of the sights and sounds of the explosion flooded back. The urge to pee overcame him, and as he struggled to extract himself from the comforter, he wondered which came first. Did the sound of the wind and rain against the window convince him he had to go, or did the urge to go wake him to the sound of the wind and rain? Either way, he had to go. *Now*.

The numbers on the clock read 2:36 when he returned to bed. Calculating another five hours of sleep awaited, he flicked on the bedside lamp, retrieved his striped pajamas from his gym bag, and changed into them. He left his socks on as another layer of protection against whatever might hide in the carpet and pulled the covers to mid-chest level. The room had warmed, even though the air conditioner chugged to life every so often. He immediately fell asleep again.

The clock read 8:14 the next time he woke. Light filtered into the room around the edges of the curtain. He got up and pushed them aside enough to see the rain, backlit by a streetlight, teeming down in sheets, and dappling the puddles glistening in the parking lot. An eighteen-wheeler took up several spaces at the side of the lot. Rivulets of water poured down the gleaming side of the sleek white trailer. The building's security lights, whose sensors must not realize daylight had arrived, reflected in the standing water while a car pulled away with its wipers flip-flopping across the windshield.

Jake used the facilities and searched for the TV remote on the desk. He clicked the TV on and pulled the chair away from the desk for a better angle. He changed the channel to the morning show on the local station he often watched at home. Glancing at the clock, he realized the news wouldn't be on for two more minutes, giving him enough time to brew some coffee.

As expected, the explosion headlined the abbreviated Saturday morning news. A tall, thin, young man wearing large, black-framed glasses and a red, hooded rain jacket with the station's logo on the pocket broadcast at the end of the street a full block from where the explosion occurred. One hand gripped an umbrella that the wind threatened to flip inside out while the other held a soggy looking, long, black microphone. The downpour dampened his face despite the umbrella, reminding Jake of reporters who leaned into a hurricane pummeling a coastal town. Jake tilted forward, his elbows on his knees, as he listened to the journalist describe the explosion. He winced and withdrew his elbows when he put pressure on his injured knee. A quick check told him the wound was still open and oozing. Water gurgled in the kettle in the background.

The reporter said above the sound of the tapping drops on his umbrella, "Jason, if you can just pan down toward the site." The camera turned away from the reporter and toward the pile of rubble. A handful of workers in yellow rain jackets and glistening hard hats scrambled over the wreckage with shovels in hand. They would step aside as a front-end loader shuffled bricks around in the pile. A police officer held the leash of a wet-furred German Shepherd as it shoved its nose into gaps in the bricks. Jake gulped. *A cadaver dog.* Another officer appeared to control a drone flying overhead in the rain. Wire fencing walled off the affected houses to the end of the block in both directions. Two ambulances sat with their lights flashing on the street in front of the house.

"As you can see, we can't get near the scene right now as the police have evacuated the houses on either side and across the street and cordoned off the area. We are told the explosion displaced fourteen families until the fire and police departments confirm it's safe for them to re-enter their homes. We don't have an indication at this time of how long that will be. The odor of gas that lingered in the air after the blast last night is not noticeable now, and I'm told by fire officials that the danger of additional explosions has passed.

"The rain has helped put out any remaining hotspots and, as you can see, workers are sorting through the rubble, hoping to find someone alive. We're told by the police department, however, that it is a recovery effort now. The dog appears to be searching for bodies. The recovery team discovered one additional body, but the police department has not released the names of the two confirmed deceased, pending notification of their next of kin. We are told that experts from the Ontario Fire Marshall's Office in Toronto will arrive on the scene today to determine the cause of the blast. We'll provide more information as it becomes available. Back to you at the station."

Jake stared at the head and shoulders of the newscaster speaking behind a desk without hearing the next item. *Another fatality!* He knew there would be more as he recalled the morning breakfast. The owner and his wife worked in the kitchen. The owner chatted up the renters at breakfast while he served their meals. That could account for the two fatalities, but Jake remembered others around the breakfast table saying in response to his question that they would stay that night. Idle chatter that likely no one would remember thirty minutes after it ended. Since the explosion occurred around eleven o'clock, all the renters were probably already in bed. He feared the final number of dead would grow, maybe by a lot.

He shook himself out of his stupor and made a cup of coffee. The first sip suggested it was tolerable, so he carried it into the bathroom and set it on the counter. The large, rectangular mirror over the counter reflected dark circles under his eyes from the night's events, making him, at least in his view, appear older than his mid-fifties. His blonde hair seemed grayer and less abundant each time he looked, undoubtedly magnified by the fact it stuck out in all directions as if an electrocution had occurred during the night. As he removed his pajamas and socks, the mirror reminded him he needed to exercise more and eat less. He stroked his whiskered chin as he thought about the personal trainer he worked with for a few months. While he made progress, he slacked off with the exercise routine, and his muffin top reflected it. He figuratively patted himself on the back for playing pickleball but remembered the beer and wings. There was another solution to all this. Stop looking in the mirror. He took a lengthy shower and dressed in the jeans and plain rust-colored tee shirt from his gym bag.

With his coffee finished, he pulled on a jacket and sauntered down the hall past the closed numbered doors. The crusty remains of a room service breakfast lay on a serving dish at one door. The same haggard clerk, looking like she pulled an all-nighter, spoke in a loud, agitated tone on the phone to someone obviously giving her a hard time. She was a large woman with curly blonde hair and brown eyes. As he watched the woman talk on the phone, he noticed a smile was never far from her lips, even under the circumstances.

A pile of local newspapers sat at the end of the counter. He caught the attention of the clerk, who nodded at his raised eyebrow as he pointed at the newspaper. He grabbed the top one and carried it to one of two blue fabric armchairs sitting behind a low table. The headline blared, *"Explosion Rips Through Westboro Neighborhood."*

A quick scan of the paper divulged nothing new from the morning TV report. A photo of the flattened B&B accompanied the article. Jake checked the byline and nodded. The article was written by Janice Richardson, the woman Jake mentored when she first joined the newspaper. The woman who became a friend. His former reporter's mind knew that Janice would have had to scramble to make sure the explosion made it into the paper, and while the details were scanty, she did her job. She would dig, and more information would appear in tomorrow's paper. A sense of pride flushed through Jake at the job Janice did.

He returned the paper, nodded to the clerk, who smiled thinly as she spoke into the phone. The slashing rain hit him in the face as soon as he opened the door. He bent into the wind, hurrying to his car, and wiped his wet face with his sleeve after he climbed in. Like magic, the deluge let up enough that his automatic wipers only swished across the window every few seconds as he drove to Brew and Buns, where his friends would discuss something inane while bragging that they were solving the world's problems. The low-hanging clouds still made for a gray day and showed no signs of giving way to sunshine soon. Jake found a parking spot half a block from Brew and Buns on Wellington Street. He retrieved the old umbrella he always carried in the car and hustled toward the plain, light brown, all-brick building.

The dripping patio chairs in front of the restaurant sat propped against drenched tables. An assortment of multicolored marigolds, tulips, and daisies in the planters by the sidewalk hung bedraggled now, but Jake knew they would thrive when the sun reappeared. The new owner, Amanda, had obviously not had time to replant an area where ignorant passersby had ripped some out during the night the week before. She had threatened to replace them with plastic flowers. A neon sign hanging on the wall above the large window overlooking the patio announced the restaurant's name in clean, tall, straight lettering.

Jake shook his umbrella at the entrance. His friends occupied the same chairs at the same table by the linear wall fireplace where they sat almost every Saturday for several years. Sometimes, someone beat them to the table but rarely. Amanda hadn't made many changes to the place other than replacing the modern art that hung on the walls with paintings for sale by local artists. The old, converted warehouse needed some color, and the paintings continued to provide it. Jake loved the contemporary and industrial styling mix and always enjoyed meeting the group for breakfast. In fact, he credited it as the one thing that maintained his sanity when Mia died. Well, that and the fact he became very close in the last few months with the only female in the breakfast group, Detective Dani Perez.

Jake always expected Amanda to change the name of the restaurant after she took over. "Brew and Buns" referred to the amazing coffee and delicious cinnamon rolls the patrons enjoyed, but Eric Jacobson, the breakfast gathering's organizer, always teased the previous owner about the name. "It could be a strip joint," he'd say before laughing uproariously. He hadn't said the same thing to Amanda, to Jake's knowledge, but she must have heard Eric mention it before.

Jake exchanged nods with two men and two women who also seemed to be there every Saturday on his way to his usual spot between Eric Jacobson and Dani's empty chair. He said, "Good morning" to the group and Pierre Chevrier, the only French-Canadian in the gathering, responded by saying, "We never worry about Jake showing up for breakfast because it's, well, breakfast. Even if he shows up late, huh, Jake?" The short, stout, and balding former bus driver added with a chuckle, "Hot date again last night, Jake? It looks like she scratched your face pretty good."

Jake had learned to accept the weekly barbs coming from Chevrier. Everyone knew Jake and Dani had openly become an item, so the "hot date" comment referred to that. He usually batted the comments aside with some large new word nobody ever used that he picked up at home from his electronic assistant, Alexa. He listened to the daily word of the day, and he had a good one he planned to slip in today when he got the chance. The lawyer and most athletic of the group, Ryan Cambridge, glanced at him expectantly as if waiting for it.

Amanda, who was in her twenties and well-respected by the group, came along with the coffee pot. Jake rested his chin on his hand so the scratch wouldn't be so prominent, and he noticed Ryan's cup was half full. He nudged the lawyer. "You must have been here for a while. You're almost ready for a second cup."

Amanda filled the cups around the table and topped up Ryan's. "I assume everyone wants the usual?" she said.

Everyone nodded and thanked her. They had all been coming long enough that she remembered their preferences. Jake occasionally threw a spanner into the works by asking for a yogurt parfait, but the scent of bacon in the room, like a seductive come-hither perfume, became too much to resist.

A recent heart attack changed Eric's diet. A well-worn, ragged Montreal Expos hat covered the retired public servant's bald head, and, to his credit, he had dropped several pounds. Amanda knew his new order was simply toast and decaffeinated coffee. He asked the group, "Did everyone read about the explosion last night? That's scary. Jake, you must've heard it. It wasn't far from your place."

Jake considered his friend and realized how he changed since the weight loss. His complexion became smoother and livelier, and the weight change erased several lines from his face. Jake and Eric had been friends at school. Some of their schoolmates bullied Eric about his weight and the way his mouth turned down at the corners, which always gave him a sullen appearance. Jake took care of one tormentor with a well-placed punch to his ear. If only they could see Eric now.

Jake said, "I was staying at that Bed and Breakfast. Another few minutes and the explosion would have buried me under the rubble." As all eyes widened around the table to large white orbs, he explained his reason for staying at the B&B and everything that had transpired the night before to the stunned group. Eyes stared, and mouths gaped as he recounted the story. He finished by saying, "The officer asked me to go to the police station this afternoon for another interview and to diagram the route of the car that nearly hit me. At least, what I know of it."

Ryan spoke first. "At least, now we know what happened to your chin. Surely, they don't suspect murder. Somebody would have to have done something crazy to anger someone else enough to murder a bunch of people. Why not just wait and run that person down when they left the B&B? Maybe the driver of the car thought you were someone else."

Jake sat back as he stared at Ryan. "Huh, that's an excellent theory. I don't think anyone is suggesting murder. The car is suspicious, but it could have been coincidence. The gas smell at the scene suggested a leak. You've probably seen the pictures. The house looked a lot like the gas leak explosions on TV. There wasn't much left of the house. It happened so fast, leaving total devastation in the area. I can't imagine anyone surviving."

"Any idea how many are dead?" This from Pierre.

"I know about the four people I had breakfast with, plus the owner and his wife, but I have no idea who was there when the blast happened. People may have checked in and out during the day. The newspaper confirmed two dead this morning."

They talked more about the explosion, tossing around theories about why it could've happened. Eric said natural gas scared him and that he heated his house with electricity. He added, "I even barbecue the old-fashioned way with briquets."

After discussing the time required for briquets to heat, all three offered Jake a place to stay and admonished him for not asking. Pierre said, "You could always stay with Dani, huh, Jake?" Jake ignored the barb and said he didn't want to put anyone out and that he felt comfortable at the hotel. As breakfast arrived, the conversation switched to lighter topics. Jake listened as he chewed. Eric, who played bass guitar all his life, spoke of practicing with his classic rock band again after recovering from his heart attack. Ryan, who played hockey during the winter in a beer league, talked about the mixed-gender, slow-pitch baseball team he joined. Sports, travel, and electric cars all got some attention. Pierre tried to get a reaction from Jake on various subjects. At one point, Jake suggested to Pierre that he should try to be more luculent.

Eric and Ryan nodded sagely as if they knew what the word meant. Jake imagined a giant question mark where Pierre's face should be. Pierre stopped talking.

As Amanda cleared the dishes from the table, Jake glanced at his watch and said, "Sorry guys, I must go. The police station awaits."

"Police station?" Amanda said. "Are you in trouble with the law again, Jake?" She noticed his face for the first time and said with a chuckle, "Because of the barroom brawl you were in last night?"

As Jake tapped the keys on the machine to add a tip and pressed his card against the screen to pay, he recounted the story again in a few sentences.

Just as the others had done, Amanda's eyes widened as she balanced four plates in her hand and on her arm while taking back the machine with the other hand. When Jake finished his story, she said, "I didn't hear about the explosion, but I smelled smoke in the air this morning. I assumed it was from some wildfire somewhere. I'm exhausted when I get home and fall into bed. No time to listen to the news. I'm glad you're alright, Jake. Take care of yourself, okay? I don't want to lose one of my best customers."

As they got up to leave, Eric and Ryan hung back as Pierre headed for the door. Ryan said, "You can tell us now. What does luc…whatever that word was that you used on Pierre mean?"

Jake chuckled. "It means to express yourself clearly. I write words down I get from Alexa's word of the day. It's fun to toss them out to Pierre to shut him up."

As the threesome headed for the entrance laughing, Pierre stood at the door with the vacant look of a man who didn't understand what was going on.

CHAPTER FIVE

JAKE'S CAR SLUICED through the rain that had started again and splashed through the puddles as he drove to his house to throw the previous night's clothes that lay on the laundry room's floor into the washing machine. The odor from the floors had decreased significantly, but he still didn't feel comfortable staying at the house. While his clothes soaked, he adjusted some of the furniture that didn't end up exactly where it belonged after the floor refinishing before driving to the nearest Walmart to shop for a new razor and other toiletries. His shopping included salve and band-aids to put on his knee and chin. Back at the house, he moved his freshly washed clothes from the washing machine to the dryer. His knee was more bruised than anything, so a single band-aid covered the wound, and he applied salve to his chin.

Around two p.m., he called Dani.

After exchanging pleasantries and relieving Dani's concerns about his state of mind and health, he said, "Is this a good time to come to the station?"

"Yes, text me when you're done."

Jake took about ten minutes to drive to the station on Elgin Street and park. He handed the piece of paper with the case number to the receptionist, who ushered him into the interior of the building and introduced him to a constable named Lisa Stouten. Jake thought she seemed small for a police officer, but he imagined she could handle herself. She appeared to be in her thirties and well-muscled. Tanned arms protruded from her blouse. She wore her blonde hair pulled back in a severe bun, and she walked ramrod straight with purpose. She pointed Jake to the nearest office and told him to take a seat.

Lisa sat at the desk, opened his case file on the computer, and asked him to tell his story. His retelling remained unchanged from the story he told the officer the night before, but he added two more pickleball players' names to the list of people who could verify his whereabouts. Constable Stouten asked him to diagram where he was when the car nearly hit him and the direction it came from, which he did to the best of his ability.

When Stouten finished with him, he texted Dani to see where she wanted to meet. She surprised Jake when she suggested they meet in her car in the basement. She told him the section of the garage where she parked. He took the elevator to the lower level and wandered to the section of the garage she told him about. Stagnant air greeted him when he walked through the door to the dimly lit garage. Concrete walls surrounded the area with numbered pillars every few feet. Police cars and unmarked vehicles filled many of the spaces. Painted pipes and cables criss-crossed the ceiling.

Jake saw no sign of Dani until an arm waved out the window of a marked Ford Explorer in the garage's corner. When he arrived at the SUV and climbed in the passenger side, he said, "Well, this is clandestine. Like Jack Ryan meeting a lovely informant on the streets of Prague. To what do I owe this special treatment?"

Dani's facial expression remained unchanged, and her appearance alarmed Jake. Maybe poor lighting in the garage contributed, but her olive skin appeared paler than usual, and strands of dark hair poked in different directions. Her luminous eyes were puffy and drooped from fatigue. It was an unusual look for the normally well-kempt Dani. Jake surmised she had slept little in the last twenty-four hours.

Jake said, "Are you okay? Looks like you could use some sleep."

"Yeah, the case in the Market kept me up all night. I'm going home to sleep for a few minutes after we talk, but I wanted to discuss the explosion with you first. Tell me about breakfast, though. It will bring a little normalcy into my life. I imagine you covered all the usual topics. Let's see. Music. Cars. Travel. Sports. Am I missing anything? Did you miss my usual outstanding contribution to raising the level of the conversation? Oh, and I assume Pierre made some stupid comment to you."

"I always miss you when you can't attend, Dani. You know that. We covered all those things, but we also talked about the explosion. They were all aghast to hear I could have been killed in the blast." A chuckle escaped Jake's lips. "Gives me the impression they care. Even Pierre was concerned." A wry smile crossed his lips before he continued. "You've become very protective of me with Pierre lately. He's a good guy deep down inside. He was there for Eric when he suffered from a heart attack. Sometimes, we just have to scrape through the gruff exterior. So, is the explosion an official homicide investigation?"

"No, I have no reason to believe it's a homicide other than the car, so any investigation is unofficial. That's why we're meeting here. How many people were staying at the B&B?"

Jake had covered this ground a few times already, but he thought back again to his breakfast at the B&B. "The owner and his wife. They appeared to be Middle Eastern. A Caucasian man and his wife in their mid-thirties sat at the table. Most appeared to be roughly the same age. I was the old man in the group. A man sat at the end of the table. Also, Caucasian. Didn't say a word, other than to mumble he was an accountant when I asked what he did. I wouldn't be asking him to do my books. I guess nobody will now. He wolfed down his meal and left. He kind of hunched over when he stormed away, like he had a sore back. The last person was a pretty young woman. I remember her first name was Willow. She said very little. Just that she was looking for a job. It's kind of an unusual name, so it stuck with me. Don't ask for any other names. I've tried to remember, but I'm drawing a blank."

Dani frowned. "Huh, that's interesting." She didn't elaborate on her comment. "So far, the only thing that looks suspicious is the car that nearly ran you down. I'm sure an investigator is checking security camera footage to find out who the car belongs to. They'll also check your story. I have no official role in the case, and anyway, we're stretched to the limit. If I had the resources, I would assign one of them to investigate the backgrounds of the deceased for any reason someone would want one of them dead. Pretty drastic to take out a bunch of people for the sake of murdering one, though. Fortunately, the owner kept a manual register of the renters, which the firefighters found. The computer was unsalvageable. The fire destroyed most of the paper copy, but the list of the day's renters was legible. There were four names on the list. You were the fourth. There was the married couple and Willow. The owner and his wife have been located. All are pending notification of next of kin. The official word so far is that it's a gas explosion, but the timing of the speeding car is suspicious."

Jake gulped. So many people! Maybe some of them escaped, he hoped.

"The guys and I talked about the fact that murder is unlikely. Why would anyone blow up a house to kill one person? They would have to be desperate. Or insane. It's surprising the owner kept a manual register in this day and age." Then, he tightened his lips and nodded as a thought struck him. "I wrote an article for the paper before I retired about the underground economy. It's not uncommon for businesses to keep two sets of records. One for themselves and an official one for the taxman. If that's the case, I wonder which one the paper copy is. I suspect it's the right one with all the information. It would be easier to destroy. So, you probably know the right number of people staying there, which means Mr. Grumpy accountant checked out. The computer log might have had a lower number. Someone could pay cash, which the owners would pocket." Jake stopped, realizing he was visualizing out loud. "Anyway, you said you might need my help with something. You know I'm always happy to get involved."

Dani nodded.

"Oh, yes, I know. I've seen the trouble you get into, remember? I could get in trouble, too, if I shared details of the explosion with you, so I'm not about to do that." She abruptly changed the subject. "Did I ever show you how one of these works?" She pointed to the computer mounted to the dash that Jake knew held, or had access to, incredible amounts of data used by police officers. "We're trained to be careful when someone is in the car because if, say, a private citizen pressed that key, they would know as much as we do."

Jake sat and waited. He knew Dani tried to tell him something without telling him to avoid jeopardizing her career. It became clear when Dani said, "I drank too much coffee today. I need to run to the washroom. Be right back."

Jake watched Dani exit the car and hustle toward the door to the building. He admired her as she walked. The woman had a way of exciting Jake just by breathing. It was an amazing feeling. When she disappeared through the door, he pressed the key she had pointed to, lighting up the computer screen. He sat, stunned, as he read the page the computer opened to. It displayed a photo of the list of the known people at the B&B the morning of the explosion. But Dani was right. Only six names appeared on the list, including his. Jake attributed each name to the people he knew to be there. The name of the silent accountant at the end of the table wasn't there.

CHAPTER SIX

JAKE REALIZED HE had no time to ponder the anomaly, so he fumbled in his pocket for his phone. He thought of the kids who could retrieve their phone and snap a photo in seconds, able to catch a disaster in the making or in progress, almost as if they had advance knowledge of its occurrence. They would post it on social media for the world to see in the blink of an eye. Dani's daughter, Emilie, could do that. Hell, Jake thought, even his own daughter, Avery, in her late twenties, could do that. Jake couldn't do that.

Once he retrieved his phone, he had to punch in his password and swipe the screen until he located the camera icon. He stopped swiping when he remembered it was on the first page. Centering the computer screen on his phone display presented another difficulty for the technically challenged Jake. He felt a hundred years old. When he got his finger out of the sight line of the lens and tapped the round red button in the center at the bottom to take the photo, he resolved to talk to Avery about simplifying this entire process. There must be an easier way. He thought about how much easier life would have been during his reporter days if he'd had a modern-day phone to record interviews and take pictures. Of course, deadlines would have been even tighter than they were in his day. The bosses would have expected reports instantaneously. Maybe, he decided, things were better in his day. He tapped the key on the police computer again to return it to its sleep state.

Jake glanced through the front windshield as Dani opened the door through which she exited and strode toward the car. When she climbed into the driver's side, she regarded him with a wry smile. "You're frowning. Everything okay?" she asked innocently.

"Yes, of course," Jake replied. He realized Dani was glancing at the phone in his hand. He returned the phone to his pocket.

"Well, if everything's okay, I must get back to work. I'll call you when I get a minute. I'm hoping to spend time with Emilie tonight." Dani leaned across the seat for a kiss that Jake happily provided.

Jake exited the car and rode the elevator to the ground floor as he considered the names on the list. He recognized the owner's name, Omar Demir. Omar never introduced his wife, who shared the kitchen with her husband, but now Jake knew her name was Seda Demir. Omar did the serving and chatted about Ottawa with his guests. Jake recalled being introduced to the couple seated across from him at the table but didn't recall their names. Now, he knew them to be Francis and Craig Thorpe, and he remembered Craig worked with the military. He said that Francis worked in retail. She never said much. They lived on the Canadian Forces Base in Petawawa, Ontario. The other person on the list was Willow Altman, the young woman who said she was unemployed. He recalled her as being down, despondent.

The problem was the other person sitting at the end of the table for breakfast. The man had not been approachable, to say the least. He grunted a response to Jake's morning greeting and kept his head down throughout the meal, shoveling food into his mouth as if afraid someone would steal it. He showed no interest in taking part in the casual conversation with Jake, the Thorpes, or the owners, other than mumbling that he worked as an accountant. About halfway through his meal, he scraped his chair back, stood, threw his napkin on his plate, and left. Everyone kept their heads down, not even acknowledging his departure. Lucky for him, he may have left the B&B before it blew up. The man's name did not appear on the list of registered guests, and apparently, no one else checked in or out during the day.

Jake tried to recall the conversation around the table. He remembered asking the Thorpes what they planned to do in Ottawa. Francis said they planned to sightsee and shop. Willow said she was looking for a job. That was it. The rest of the conversation circled around the weather and their respective experiences during the pandemic. It was a quiet group.

Jake opened his umbrella to walk to his car, but the rain had settled down to a whimper as only light showers stippled the surface of the sidewalk. As he drove back to the hotel, he thought about the mystery man at the end of the table. A problem seemed to weigh heavily on the man. *Could it be something serious enough that someone wanted him dead? Or could he have been plotting the demise of everyone else in the room?*

Jake pulled into the parking lot at the hotel. He shook out the open umbrella in the parking lot and greeted a slim, tanned man in his forties smoking a cigarette at the side entrance to the hotel. The man stood taller than Jake, his shaggy brown hair hanging over his ears. He wore a gray jacket, tight across his brawny chest, with a white electrician company's name stitched on the right arm and matching work pants. He nodded back and observed as Jake closed the umbrella and held the key card to the reader. The door buzzed open, and Jake sauntered to his room door, where he repeated the process with the card. Once inside, he hung his coat on the hanger to give it a chance to dry and set the open umbrella on the floor. He boiled water in the kettle as he remembered for the 100th time that he should reduce his coffee intake.

After the kettle finished gurgling and he fixed a cup to his liking, he sat in the single armchair in the room and dialed his daughter, Avery, in Toronto. The phone rang over and over. Jake expected it to go to voice mail when she breathlessly picked up.

"Hi, Dad." An electronic hiss on the line nearly drowned out what she said.

"Sweetie, I'm going to hang up and try this again. I can barely hear you." Jake dialed again. This time, she picked up right away.

"Hi! That's better. I just came through the door when I heard the phone ringing in my pocket. Nick and I were out picking up groceries. My hands were full, so I had to set everything down before I answered. I planned to call you. I read about that awful explosion in the news. That was close to your place, wasn't it?"

Jake hesitated, wondering how much he should tell his daughter. Recent involvement in Dani's cases made Avery nervous. He needed her help, so he was partly truthful. He told her about narrowly missing the explosion but left the car that almost hit him and the resulting bruises out of his story.

Avery remained calm. Jake's narrow escapes from adventures had become commonplace even though she didn't like it. "You seem to be a trouble magnet since you retired. Maybe you should go back to work. Find a job at a small-town newspaper to keep you busy. I'm glad you're not hurt, at least. I assume it was a gas explosion. We had one in Toronto recently. They're so scary. The explosion flattened the house, but no one was home when it happened, thank God."

Jake took a sip of his steaming coffee, burning his lips before he replied, "I like your suggestion about the small-town newspaper job, but they're all closing. They don't seem to be profitable anymore. Everyone reads the so-called news on the internet now, although it's often sensationalism and opinion written to spark controversy. People would rather read opinion than fact. Anyway, don't get me started about that. They're calling the blast a gas explosion for now, but the Fire Marshall will come from Toronto to confirm it. There were fatalities. That reminds me, I wanted to ask something related to the explosion."

"That's so sad about the fatalities." Avery waited a beat and then said, "Before you ask your question, and on a happier note, I want to share some news with you. I'm bursting to tell you, so let me go first, okay?"

Jake set aside his question for Avery for the moment. He always loved news from his daughter. "What is it, dear?" he asked.

"Well, Nick and I wanted to come up to Ottawa to tell you, but we're busy for the next few weekends. Nick has a series of webinars he's giving on Saturdays, and I couldn't wait to let you know."

Jake's curiosity rose as his daughter doled out the tidbits of information. He blew on his coffee and took a drink. After a few agonizing seconds, she made her announcement.

"Dad, we're expecting."

CHAPTER SEVEN

JAKE WAS FORTUNATE he had swallowed his coffee before hearing the news, or he would have been wiping it off the television screen. He spilled some on his pants as his heart skipped a beat. Did he hear right? He remained silent as a thousand thoughts crashed into each other in his head.

My little girl is having a baby.
She's not old enough, is she?
Wait, I'm going to be a grandfather?
Am I old enough for that?
This doesn't seem possible.

"Dad, are you okay?" Avery chuckled on the other end of the line. "You're going to be a grandfather! This might be a shock to you, but Nick and I have been talking about getting pregnant for some time now. I went off the pill a while ago. We're so excited."

Whoa, Jake thought. She went off the pill!? That qualified as T.M.I. *Too much information.*

"Uh, congratulations, honey. That is exciting," Jake managed. He squeezed his eyes together and wrinkled his nose, knowing his voice sounded unconvincing. He took a deep breath and tried again. "I wish your mom could be here to share the excitement." He wondered what else he should say. *What do fathers say at a time like this?* Oh, yes, "What's the due date?"

"Unless it's early, it will be a January baby. Early January. We're hoping for after Christmas. It doesn't seem fair to share its birthday with Christmas. Oh, Dad, I'm so excited!"

"I can tell, sweetie, and I'm excited for you." Jake decided to take a bit of time to absorb the information. In his mind, two minutes ago, his daughter was his baby girl, and now, in a few months, she would be a mother. Yes, this would take a bit of getting used to.

"I'll travel to Toronto soon to check up on you and Nick. Maybe I'll take the train. I enjoyed riding the rails last time."

"It would be great to see you, Dad. Like I said, work has swamped Nick lately, and I don't have many holidays left. I'd like to save them for Christmas, so if you come down, it would be awesome. Oh, wait, you said you had something to ask me."

Jake forgot the original reason for his call as he processed the news about his expectant daughter. His mind snapped back to the explosion. He wasn't sure how to ask since Avery wasn't a fan of him getting involved in investigations. However, this time Dani asked him to get involved, so the discussion might go better. He plunged ahead.

"Honey, Dani asked me to investigate the backgrounds of the people who stayed at the Bed and Breakfast when I left in the morning. I have a list of names, but since you're a little savvier than me with social media, I'm hoping you can suggest an approach. I know there's Linked something and a few others I can check. Can you point me in the right direction?"

His suggestion that Avery was "a little savvier" momentarily sidetracked his daughter, which he intended.

Avery's words road out of her mouth on the wave of a chuckle. "*A little savvier*!? Dad, you could put your knowledge of social media in a thimble."

Jake's ruse didn't last long.

"But what's this about getting involved again? Now Dani's a co-conspirator!? I'm going to chat with her. I get why you always get into trouble. You go looking for it."

"It's not like that, honey. This time, Dani wants me to help. She's involved in another case, and they don't consider the explosion a homicide. She wants to get a leg up in case it becomes a homicide investigation, and she doesn't have the resources to do it. I'm just helping a friend."

"Okay, two things, Dad. Dani is more than a 'friend,' and it's time you two agreed on that and started acting accordingly. Second, why is there the remotest possibility that this could be more than a gas explosion?"

Jake slumped back in his chair, thankful he chose not to make a video call. Sometimes it was better when his daughter couldn't see his face. He realized he hadn't told Avery about the car that almost hit him as a crimson flush raced up his neck and overwhelmed his face.

He ignored the comment about Dani and told Avery about the car without going into detail. "It's probably coincidence that the car nearly hit me, but you know Dani. She's nothing if she's not proactive. So, she wants me to investigate the social media accounts of the people who stayed at the B&B."

A long sigh came from the other end of the phone. "Dani's good for you, Dad, but I wish she would stop dragging you into these things. I just know you'll get into trouble because you won't let it go. If I don't help you, you'll find another way to get involved. Dog with a bone comes to mind. I can't help you track them down, but I'll tell you the social media I'm aware of. Do you have a pen?"

Jake scrounged in the desk for a pen and paper and scribbled as Avery rattled off a list of social media sites. He was familiar with Facebook and Instagram, but he shook his head as the list lengthened. Something called 'X,' formerly known as Twitter, and Facebook had become Meta. *How does anyone keep up?* It would be a full-time job feeding the monsters. It was enough to make his head explode.

Jake shook his head as he marveled at the length of the list and thanked Avery. He congratulated her again on the impending arrival of the baby and disconnected the call. He had his work cut out for him, that's for sure... after he came to grips with his new title of "Grandfather in Waiting."

CHAPTER EIGHT

JAKE'S EYES STARED unseeing at the phone he had just set on the desk. The pregnancy news stunned him. He supposed on some level, he knew this day would come, but Avery was still his little girl. Then, he remembered her excitement. He leaned back in the chair, thrust his legs out in front of him with his feet crossed, and clasped his fingers together behind his head.

Huh! I'm going to be a grandpa. Wait until Dani and the guys at breakfast hear about this. Eric is always talking about his grandkids and showing us pictures. Well, move over, Eric. There's about to be a new grandpa in town.

Jake chuckled. He couldn't wait for the next breakfast gathering, and Dani had to hear the news right away. Well, after another sip of coffee. But he grimaced as the formerly steaming coffee that touched his lips had gone cold. The coffee sat in the paper cup on the desk long enough that any hint of heat was long gone. He slipped the cup into the microwave and set the timer for forty seconds. When the beep announced it was done, he retrieved the cup and dialed Dani's number. The call went directly to voice mail. He decided it would be fun to leave her a cryptic message, although the lack of information would agitate her.

"Hi, Dani, it's Jake." He thought that was stupid since she would recognize him as soon as she heard his voice. "I talked to Avery, and she had exciting news to share. Call me when you can. Hope you're having a good day chasing the bad guys."

He disconnected the call and stood from the chair to stretch, deciding that hotels must buy their chairs in bulk from the lowest bidder. At least this one did. He wandered into the bathroom to wipe the coffee stains from his pants and looked in the mirror. There were wrinkles, for sure, and gray streaks appearing in his hair. His chest sagged much more than in his youth, and his belly matched. Pickleball made him breathe hard. He silently queried the mirror. *Am I old enough to be a grandpa?* He imagined the mirror answering back. *Is that a rhetorical question? Just look at yourself.*

Wiping his pants with a damp cloth didn't help the coffee stain, so he wandered back to the room and dug a fresh pair of blue jeans from his bag. Deciding it would be much more convenient to write on a print copy of the list of contacts, he strolled to the front desk. Pointing to a computer station in the corner, he asked, "Is that computer connected to a printer somewhere I can access?"

The rumpled desk clerk nodded. "Is your document on a memory stick? You can just plug the stick into the computer and ask it to print."

"I don't have a stick. There's a document on my phone. I suppose I could email it to myself, save it, and print it, right?"

The desk clerk chuckled. "Yes, but why don't we connect your phone to the printer? I can give you the digital location of the printer."

Jake's brow creased, and his nose wrinkled. "I could if I knew how," he said sheepishly. For the first time, he noticed the name on the woman's nametag identified her as Jen Tripley.

Jen said, "I can help with that." She nodded toward a printer behind her. Within seconds, she connected the printer to Jake's phone and printed off the document with the names. "Just don't go printing some novel or something." She laughed. "Paper's expensive, and sometimes when someone else refills the paper tray, they don't attach the catcher thing properly, so the printed stuff goes all over the floor. We wouldn't want that now, would we?"

Jake agreed they wouldn't and took the printed sheet back to his room. He sat in the chair in front of the desk examining the names. Omar and Seda Demir. Craig and Francis Thorpe. Willow Altman. Beside Omar and Seda, Jake wrote "owners." He noted "military, Petawawa" beside Craig's name, and "retail clerk" beside Francis's name. He added "unemployed" beside Willow's name. At the end of the list, he wrote "accountant" with a question mark beside it.

Jake set the list on the laptop keyboard and sat staring at it with his elbow on the arm of the chair and his thumb and index finger gently tugging and releasing his bottom lip. He didn't recall any sense of familiarity among the group. They didn't seem to know each other, and why would they? They were in town for different reasons. Nothing suggested any of them was involved in anything untoward. Everything seemed innocent and aboveboard. The only thing to suggest something amiss was the car that nearly ran him down, and that could have been an accident. The night was dark, and he was jaywalking halfway across the street when the car came blasting around the corner. Sure, the driver went too fast, but that's not uncommon. There could be a million explanations for the accountant's surliness. He could have fought with his wife or girlfriend.

Jake did as Dani asked. He needed something to occupy his time, anyway, so why not check out the social media accounts as she suggested? Just as Dani popped into his mind, his cell phone rang, and the screen displayed her name.

"Hi, Dani," he said. "How's your case going?"

"It's okay. We'll get him. How're you making out with the social media for the people staying at the B&B?"

"I've just started. I spoke with Avery for a few minutes, and she gave me some exciting news. She's…"

"Pregnant," Dani finished Jake's sentence.

Jake took in a breath. "How do you *do* that?"

"Call it female intuition, dear. That's exciting news. Is she okay? Not throwing up or anything? Ice cream cravings?"

"Uh, I don't know. I didn't ask, and she didn't say. She would've told me if she wasn't okay, wouldn't she?"

Dani chuckled. "Jake, those things are common with pregnancy. Even if she were experiencing them, it would be nothing to worry about. Now, I'm sorry, but I must go. I would rather talk to you, but criminals await. We'll chat later, okay?"

"Of course, Dani. Go do what you must do. Remember, I miss you, though."

"I miss you, too, Jake. Chat later."

She hung up, leaving Jake staring at the phone. He asked himself again for the umpteenth time since he had known this amazing woman. *How does she do that?*

CHAPTER NINE

JAKE PRESSED THE space bar to wake up his laptop and started with the easy ones: the social media sites he was familiar with and the ones he assumed everyone used. A search for Seda and Omar Demir produced nothing. It was like they didn't exist, at least on the sites with which Jake was familiar. That was strange, Jake thought, although it was possible that they were just uncomfortable maintaining a presence on social media. Jake knew he wouldn't have a social media account either if it weren't for Avery.

He tapped the keys again to search for Craig Thorpe. A handful of Craig Thorpes came up. The names at the top of the list were the closest geographically, but the third from the top stood out. The photo displayed the man he met... the man who probably lay dead in a morgue somewhere now. Jake didn't want to even consider the shape the man's body might be in.

He noted on the list that Thorpe had three friends on the social media site. Three! He checked Thorpe's posts to identify those who liked them the most. Nobody. No posts. He checked the three friends; they all seemed local to the military base. Maybe, he thought, he should start with them if Dani wanted him to carry this any further. He jotted their names down on his sheet.

Next, he searched for Craig's wife, Francis. Unbelievably, the results came up the same. She had very few friends and no posts. In fact, she also had three friends, one of whom overlapped with her husband's. For people in their thirties who grew up with technology and social media, it seemed strange to Jake that none would maintain a presence online. He thought either he was wasting his time, or he was on to something.

Sifting through other sites Avery mentioned produced the same results. No presence. A search for Willow Altman's name brought up over 300 hundred friends. That was more like what he expected. He couldn't write them all down, so he identified the ones that seemed to be the closest and made notes about them. Eye fatigue overtook him. He was about to call it a night when something else occurred to him. He searched for the Sweet Dreams Bed and Breakfast. That's how he found the house. He recalled he didn't spend a lot of time reading about the house. He wanted somewhere to live for five days, and the Sweet Dreams B&B was convenient, affordable, and boasted a good star rating. That was all that mattered to him.

But spending more time on it was no more productive. The Demirs apparently purchased the house from the previous B&B owner two years' prior. The site provided background about the house and details about each of the rooms. Renters gave the B&B four and five-star ratings, which Jake decided he could follow up on if necessary. He took photos of the reviews with his phone.

A glance at the clock beside the bed told him it was 10:15. The time flew during his fruitless search. If Dani and her team did this, they would access credit card statements, utility bills, bank accounts, browser history... Things that could really tell a story about someone. But Jake could access none of that. His eyes hurt like they were full of gritty sand, and a dull ache wandered up his spine from sitting hunched over the laptop in the uncomfortable chair. Time for a break. He decided tomorrow he would move back home even though it was a day early. He could continue his search in comfort. Some of the odor from the finished hardwood floors might remain, but he was sure it would be safe enough.

He debated putting on his pajamas, turning on the TV, and going to bed, but decided he needed to stretch his legs first. He pulled on his coat and headed for the door. The hallway to the front lobby was eerily quiet except for the murmuring of a TV set behind one door.

He didn't see Jen Tripley, the front desk clerk, this time. No one stood behind the desk. Jake suspected someone was working away in the back office. He exited the front door and turned right on the sidewalk on Carling Avenue.

The humid night air after the deluge the night before and into the day weighed down on him like a wet blanket. His shirt dampened with sweat the minute he took a few steps, but he continued to walk five blocks east on Carling before he turned to come back. His phone rang as he stopped at a red light and turned to return to the hotel. The screen announced Dani.

"Hi, Dani," he said. "How are you?"

"I'm missing my life, Jake. That's how I am. I hope you weren't sleeping. We're making progress on the Market knifing incident, though." The usually emphatic Dani's voice was so soft that the sound of a passing car drowned it out. Jake pressed the phone harder to his ear and asked her to repeat what she said.

When he heard her, he said, "That's good news, Dani. Are you okay? You sound exhausted."

"Yeah, I'm okay. Exhausted is a good word for it. I need my bed and a shower, not in that order. Listen, I'm going home for some rest, but let's meet for a quick coffee somewhere. My staff is investigating the knifing, so I've got a few hours. I'll call my friend at the condo and tell her I'll be late. Emilie is staying with a friend tonight. I miss seeing you. I have news about the car that nearly ran you down, too."

"It will be nice to hear about the car, but we don't need an excuse, sweetie. Do you want to come to the hotel on the way home? The coffee isn't the best, but it's hot. The room isn't the most comfortable, but it's quiet. We could also meet at Tim Horton's on Carling if you prefer."

"No, hot swill, and a quiet, uncomfortable hotel room sounds perfect. It will differ from here. At least the quiet part. Where are you, by the way? It sounds like you're walking on a speedway."

The corners of Jake's mouth turned up in a smile at the very astute Dani. There would be no putting anything by her. He quickened his pace as the thought of seeing Dani in a few minutes energized him. At the speed she drove, she would almost be at the hotel before she hung up the phone.

"I just needed fresh air. Lots of people out and about tonight. I wanted to stretch after spending the evening researching the people at the B&B. I'll fill you in when you get here, although I don't have much to tell you."

"Okay, I'm in the car now. I'll see you soon. Oh, it would help if you gave me your room number."

Jake provided the number as he walked toward the hotel, which loomed larger with each step. When he arrived, a bus idled in front of the hotel. A huge decal of a beaming tiger decked out in a baseball uniform with a bat slung over his shoulder was plastered on the side of the bus. A group of tired-looking teen boys filled the lobby. Jen, the desk clerk, tapped on her keyboard at the counter as she spoke to an adult male. Jake overheard the man mention the Rockfort Tigers as he wove through the crowd, and most of the boys wore blue satin jackets with the team logo and the words "Little League Champs" stitched on the arm. He recalled something in the paper about the team playing in the Little League World Series last year or maybe the year before.

He hurried to his room, unlocked the door, flicked on the light switch, and filled the kettle with warm water from the tap in the sink. He opened a blue packet and dumped the grounds into his cup. Pushing the curtains aside to see if Dani had arrived in the parking lot yet produced a startling sight. Dani wheeled her car into a vacant spot in the lot. But further across the parking lot sat a dark-colored sedan. An unsettled sensation came over him. The car looked so familiar. Could it be the one that almost ran him down? No, it couldn't be. He must be imagining things.

The driver's side faced Jake, so he saw the profile of a man sitting behind the wheel in the wash of the lot's security lights. As Jake stared, the man seemed to sense he was being observed. He turned to look directly at the window where Jake stood. The hairs rose on the back of Jake's neck. The man appeared to look right through him. Even in the night's dullness and with the distance between the car and the back of the building, the familiarity extended from the car to the man. Jake decided his imagination must be running wild. There must be some lingering aftereffect from the previous night's events. He glanced to the left to see Dani hurrying toward the building.

And quickly closed the drapes.

CHAPTER TEN

ONE LAST GLANCE through the small gap in the drapes told Jake the man never took his eyes from the window. At least, that was the impression he got. From that distance, the man could be looking anywhere. But a nagging familiarity bothered Jake. A soft tap at the door caused any lingering thoughts of the man and the car to vanish.

Jake ensured the drapes overlapped to prevent anyone from looking in and hurried to the door. When he opened it, Dani stood on the other side with one eyebrow raised and her hand on a hip thrust to the side in a striking pose.

"You called for room service?" she asked in a throaty voice before bursting out laughing.

Jake joined her with a laugh of his own and stepped aside to let her in. They exchanged a hug and a lingering kiss.

Dani held Jake longer than usual. "It's so good to see you," she breathed into his ear before releasing him from the hug.

"It's good to see you, too, Dani. I've missed you. Come in. Let me take your jacket."

Jake shoved his jacket along the rod in the closet and stored Dani's dusty pink blazer beside it. As he followed her into the room, he admired her shape. She wore a white blouse and navy blue pants, which stressed her figure. As happy as he was to see Dani, Jake worried she worked too hard. She buried herself in her work sometimes. Jake understood, but he wondered if she did it to avoid having a genuine relationship. The hug was nice but almost needy. It wasn't a typical Dani hug, but then again, they agreed to go slow because of their respective previous relationships. Maybe the pressure of her job weighed on her more than usual this evening.

Dani rarely talked about her ex-husband. She avoided talking about her divorce, which made Jake wonder if she was over her marriage. But Jake had his own baggage. Thoughts of his wife, Mia, often invaded his mind since her death three years prior. Despite that, he acknowledged a natural connection with Dani. They enjoyed each other's company and missed each other when apart. They appreciated similar interests, and he deeply admired her Venezuelan spirit and determination. He was sure a heart monitor would detect his heart rate ratcheting up every time he saw her. A few months back, they took a trip to Toronto to visit his daughter, Avery, and her husband, Nick, and shared a bed. He even talked to the picture of Mia in the office at home before they left, asking for her advice. Although the photo hadn't replied, a strange calm overcame him as if Mia had given her blessing to the liaison. Jake knew Mia wouldn't believe for a second that Jake should remain alone for long.

Whenever Avery brought up his and Dani's relationship, Jake used the popular avoidance word to circumvent a protracted discussion. He told her it was "complicated." But deep down inside, he sensed he would be ready to take the next step with Dani whenever she was. He just didn't know when that would be.

Dani sat with her legs crossed on the side of the bed while Jake poured two cups of coffee. He handed one to Dani and sat in the chair opposite. "So, tell me about your day."

Dani filled him in on the ongoing investigation into the stabbing in the Byward Market. Her answers were short and to the point, like she didn't want to spend much time talking about her work. She perked up as the caffeine did its work, and she redirected the conversation to Jake's research on the B&B.

Jake said, "I didn't accomplish much, which surprised me. I found nothing about the people at the Bed and Breakfast. None of them, except Willow, has much presence on the internet. The owners have a website describing the history of the place, and several renters gave the B&B positive reviews, but they have little presence on social media. I estimate everyone except Willow was in their thirties, so you would expect they would be all over social media. They're roughly the same age as Avery, and she's posting all the time about what's going on in their lives. She posts about what she ate for breakfast. I'm sure now that she's pregnant, we're all going to be following along online until the baby is born. She has about a million friends."

Dani's mouth turned down in a frown as she raised an eyebrow at Jake.

"Okay, not a million, but you know what I mean."

Dani blew on her coffee, causing the steam to gyrate above her cup. It was a habit Jake had observed. She blew into her coffee mug until the last drop, even though it couldn't need all that cooling off. "It's strange they aren't on social media but not unheard of. There are still people that don't want to be online 24/7, but they're rare. A group of people staying at a B&B, and none of them on social media is quite the coincidence. Did you check out all the sites? There are a lot."

"Yes, Avery gave me a list. I covered most of them."

Dani blew on the last of her coffee, sipped, uncrossed her legs, and handed the empty cup back to Jake. "Well, you're right. That coffee was pretty bad," she said. She leaned back with her head resting against the headboard of the bed. As she did, her knees touched Jake's, and she didn't move them. She said, "Well, my news may remove any suspicion about the explosion. You know the car that almost ran you down? Our people looked at surveillance footage from doorbell cameras in the area and identified the license number from one of them. They traced the plate to an eighty-year-old lady who lives in the neighborhood. The Ministry of Transportation suspended her license a few weeks ago. She's legally blind and probably didn't even see you. She lives with her son and his wife and took their car for a joyride, apparently to find her husband who died a few years ago. They're putting a steering wheel lock on the car to make sure she doesn't try that again."

Jake's eyes widened, and a smile slowly crept across his lips as Dani's story unfolded. "Huh! Okay, well, so much for the getaway car theory. I don't know whether I'm happy that it wasn't the killer or sad that I might as well stop investigating. I'm glad the lady wasn't hurt."

"Yes, I'm sorry to have put you through that, although I know you like to stick your nose into things." Dani chuckled. "The Ontario Fire Marshall will be here from Toronto tomorrow. We'll get a more definitive answer about the cause of the explosion after he and his team investigate. They've found the bodies of the Demirs and Thorpes now, but there's still a pile of rubble to sift through. The heavy rain slowed things down, and most of the bricks in the house caved into the basement. No sign of Willow or the accountant, so we're hoping they checked out during the day sometime."

Jake sat thoughtfully. Then he said, "Speaking of security cameras, did they pick up the accountant coming or going? Or Willow? Didn't the Bed and Breakfast have cameras? Everyone does, nowadays, apparently. Well, except me, but I do have a security alarm, thanks to you and Avery insisting."

"No cameras at the B&B, and the ones across the street are the doorbell types that allow you to set the range. Apparently, none of the neighbors wants their cameras picking up every car on the street, and for good reason, so they narrow the range down to their doorstep. They use them to catch porch pirates, I guess. So far, no video of the accountant or anybody else coming and going."

"Okay, it sounds like the case is closed for me. I'm planning on moving home tomorrow. It's a day early, but the smell wasn't bad when I dropped in. I'll collect Oliver from you whenever it's convenient. I'm sure Emilie would like to keep him, and you would probably prefer to see him go. You should go home and get some rest."

Dan hesitated before getting up. She seemed unsettled as if

something weighed heavily on her shoulders. She grabbed her purse off the bed and drifted toward the door but stopped and turned before Jake retrieved her blazer from the closet. Dani reached for Jake and threw her arms around him, kissing him passionately. When she pulled back, she said, "Do you mind if I use your shower?"

Jake tried to hide the shocked expression on his face, but he knew Dani would see it right away. She said nothing more; just turned and walked into the bathroom, closing the door behind her. A sudden rush coursed through Jake's body like a panic attack. What should he do now? Get undressed and hop into bed? Wouldn't that be presumptuous? What if she just wanted to freshen up before driving home? What if someone from her work called while she showered to say they needed her to go in immediately? He would look like an idiot if he misinterpreted the situation and was lying naked in bed when she emerged from the bathroom, clothed and ready to work. Should he sit fully clothed, twiddling his thumbs until she came out? Would that make him appear uninterested? His heart thumped in his chest like a sledgehammer on concrete. That heart monitor he thought about earlier would blow a gasket by now. Who knew he would face these decisions in his fifties? He thought back to when he dated Mia but couldn't remember dealing with this type of situation, although it must have happened.

It was the longest eleven minutes of Jake's life. His senses seemed more acute as he heard the valve for the water in the bathroom shower shut off with a thump. He heard her voice speaking in hushed tones. She was singing or talking to someone on the phone. *Probably work.* A rustling sound followed inside the bathroom, and the hair dryer fired up. Then, the door handle rattled. Sweat popped on Jake's brow. He opted to remain fully clothed and appear casual, so he sat in the chair with his elbow resting on the desk, playing with his cell phone. The bathroom door opened with a creak, and a slight citrusy scent sifted into the room. He looked up as Dani poked her head and bare shoulders around the corner. A broad smile broke out on her face as she sauntered barefoot into the room.

She wore a white hotel towel around her body, exposing her

shoulders and shapely legs. She confidently strode toward Jake and put her hands out to pull him from the chair. Her elbows gripped the towel in place. She kissed him and then pulled away. As she did, she released the towel, letting it drop in a heap on the floor leaving her as naked as the day she was born.

Now, any doubt disappeared from Jake's mind. He understood now where this was going.

CHAPTER ELEVEN

JAKE WOKE THE next morning with his chest and torso facing Dani's back, their legs intertwined. Dani's body rose and fell against his chest. She still slept soundly. The corners of Jake's lips turned up in a satisfied smile, remembering the details of the passionate night they enjoyed. The tiny scent of citrus still lingered in the air. Tentative at first, they explored and discovered each other in a way that only a couple that are truly attracted to one another can. Knowing Dani was exhausted, Jake wanted to let her sleep, but he needed to go to the bathroom. He tried to extract his numb arm from beneath Dani's body without bothering her, but as he did, she stirred.

"Where do you think you're going?" she murmured.

"Bathroom. Go back to sleep. I'll be right back."

"Mmm, okay," Dani slurred.

But when Jake withdrew his arm, Dani bolted upright, the cover falling to her waist. "Wait, what time is it?" She glanced at the bedside clock. "Seven!? I need to go home and change and get to work."

When Jake returned, Dani still sat upright in bed with the cover pulled to her neck despite her proclamation that she wanted to leave immediately. He climbed into the bed beside her.

She said, "I decided I couldn't just take advantage of you and run. I really must go, but I wanted to tell you how much I enjoyed last night, Jake. You are very special to me, and it's something I've wanted to do since our trip. I just didn't know if you were ready to do this again."

The sound of running feet and shouting in the hallway, presumably from the teenage baseball players, came and went with the Doppler effect of a passing freight train. Jake put his arm around Dani's shoulder and pulled her tight against him. He laughed. "And I didn't know if you were ready. I'm glad you stayed."

"Well, you invited me to your hotel room."

"Uh, I agreed when you suggested it." Jake tickled Dani under the arm, and she collapsed against him in gales of laughter.

After a few minutes of playful teasing, Dani announced she really had to go. As Jake watched her dress, she said, "I must get to work, and my friend's going to ask a million questions about where I slept last night. I called her from the bathroom after I showered. She must have been able to hear the fan running, so she'll wonder what I was up to. I'll tell her the truth—that I shared a wild, passionate night with the man of my dreams, and I plan to do it over and over. She'll be jealous. She hasn't exactly had brilliant success finding the right man."

Jake reluctantly got out of bed and pulled on his clothes. "Maybe she just needs to find an overweight, balding, unemployed guy in his fifties. How could she go wrong?"

Dani pulled on the blazer Jake handed her from the closet. She said, "Well, I found mine, and I'm not sharing. And as a bonus he wears his socks to bed. Is there a particular reason? Don't get me wrong, I'm not trying to change you already. I'll save that for later." She accompanied the last sentence with an exaggerated wink.

"I'm paranoid about hotel carpets. I'm sure they're cleaned often, but you know... Believe me, I don't wear socks to bed at home. And I won't especially with my shiny new floors. Before you go, and speaking of paranoia, there's something I want to share with you. Last night, I looked out the window to see if you were in the parking lot yet, and I saw a car parked that reminded me of the one that nearly ran me down.

As I looked at the car, the driver stared at me. There was a familiarity to him I couldn't place. At least, it looked like he was staring at me. He was a long way away, so it's possible from the angle that he was looking somewhere else, but it felt like I was being watched. Maybe it was the car that triggered the familiarity. And we know now that was nothing. I don't know. The driver is probably nothing, too."

Dani frowned, pulled Jake close for a hug, and said, "A lot has happened to you in the last few days, Jake. More than anyone should have to deal with. You're not in your own home. Someone almost ran you down, and then there was the explosion that could have killed you. At least we determined that the driver of the car you saw the night of the explosion had no intention of hitting you. The Fire Marshall will determine the cause of the explosion soon, and then I hope we can move on to something else, like focusing on each other. What do you think? Sound good?"

Jake kissed her and said, "That sounds amazing. Keep me posted if you hear anything. I'm looking forward to hearing about the cause of the explosion. Please let your friend know I'll be picking up Oliver later this morning in case Emilie isn't back yet."

They kissed goodbye, and he watched Dani walk down the hall. When she turned the corner, he closed the door and leaned against it for a minute. He couldn't recall experiencing this emotional sensation for a long, long time.

CHAPTER TWELVE

JAKE SHOWERED, PULLED on his clothes, and wandered to the hotel restaurant, where he ate a leisurely breakfast of crispy bacon, two eggs over easy, and rye toast, all of which he washed down with two cups of black coffee and orange juice. He read an article in the morning paper by his friend and former colleague, Janice Richardson, with the latest updates about the explosion. It added very little other than to say that the police were still trying to notify the next of kin and would release the names in the coming days. That should spur interest from people who knew the deceased and trigger some recollections about their backgrounds. Then he remembered it didn't really matter. Dani seemed convinced the explosion was an unfortunate accident.

With Dani's news about the car and her belief the explosion probably happened accidentally, Jake was in no hurry to do anything. The checkout time posted on the door in his room said 11:00 a.m. He had packed most of his meager belongings with a plan to leave in plenty of time. He finished the last few drops of coffee and left the paper neatly folded on the table for the next people who came in. As he stood to leave, he noted patrons occupied only a few of the tables. Years in the newspaper business sharpened his observation skills, but he realized he must be slipping. He paid no attention when he arrived, but the now too familiar sensation of being watched came over him.

A gray-haired couple with a boy about twelve and a girl about ten sat at one table. The little girl sat on both hands and swung her leg like a pendulum under the table. Probably grandparents with their grandkids, he thought. Two women in business suits, both on their cell phones, sat at another. A single man in a navy suit with an open-neck white shirt watched an American news station on a TV suspended over the fireplace at a third table. But a man sitting by himself at a table near the entrance to the swinging door of the kitchen caught Jake's attention.

Jake saw the man staring at him over his mug of coffee from the corner of his eye. That's where the sensation of being observed came from. When Jake turned toward him, the man set down his coffee and nodded with a grim smile like they had been friends forever. Jake tilted his head in acknowledgment as he remembered seeing the man when he entered the hotel the first morning. He still wore the gray jacket with the name of the electrician company stitched on the arm. He realized it could have been the same man watching from the parking lot last night. Jake decided he needed to get out of there. This was getting too creepy.

He walked to the front desk and settled his bill with Jen, the clerk who never seemed to take time off, now working the cash in the restaurant as well. He glanced into the restaurant to see the man no longer sitting at the table. It was like he vanished. He said to the clerk, "I'm just curious. There was a man sitting at a table by the kitchen entrance who looked familiar to me. I can't place him, and it's going to bother me. A large man. Muscular. Shaggy, longish hair, wearing a jacket with a white electrician logo on the arm. Did you see him, or does he sound like someone staying here?"

Jen glanced toward the table Jake gestured toward and shook her head. "I pay little attention to people as they come and go. I look at them and try to act interested, but I don't really see them, you know? Except you, of course. I'll never forget the handsome stranger that didn't know how to use his phone." Her large bosom shook as she laughed.

Jake thanked her for everything, and as he hurried back to his room, he wondered again if the same man had watched him from the parking lot the night before. One thing for certain, he had to get back to his home and into his routine before his imagination drove him crazy. As he swiped the key card, he thought Dani was right. He was getting too old for everything he went through in the last few days. She said nothing about his age but pointed out he had been through a lot. She was right, as usual.

He spent the next hour reading a novel and finished packing his belongings before closing the door on the way to his car with fifteen minutes to spare. The sun's withering heat reflected off the dark pavement and hit him as soon as he exited the door leading to the parking lot. The forecast predicted a scorcher, and they got it right. He glanced around the parking lot but didn't see the dark car or the man with the electrician's jacket. The white eighteen-wheeler that took up more than its share of parking spaces, and blocked the view down the street, had left.

Jake clicked the key fob, and the doors unlocked with the familiar faint clunk. Hot air from the car smacked him in the face when he opened the door. He started the car and let the air conditioner work before driving to his house, where he dropped off his bag and picked up the cage to bring Oliver home. The familiarity of the house washed over him. Except for the faint odor of the chemicals on the floor, the house greeted him like an old friend. An old friend he hadn't spent any time with for a long time.

He drove to Dani's condo and parked in one of the guest spots at the front of the building. Emilie buzzed him in at the front door and greeted him with a smile and hug at the entrance to the condo. She met him barefoot as usual with a towel wrapped around her head and wearing an oversized pink tee shirt with a logo of a band Jake recognized for once emblazoned on the front over multicolored shorts. A pair of large white headphones reminding Jake of Mickey Mouse ears sat draped around her neck. "How ya doin', Jake?" she asked as she turned to sit at the kitchen table in front of a half-finished breakfast. A large jar of peanut butter sat with the lid off along with a knife by her plate. Her cell phone sat on the other side. She nodded at the cage Jake carried. "I see you brought Oliver's overnight bag. Want something? Orange juice or something?"

"No, I'm good, thanks. The workmen finished at my house, and the odor should be gone, so I'm moving home. I just stopped over to pick up Oliver. Where is he, by the way?"

"Probably sleeping on my bed." Emilie took a large bite from her toast and chewed vigorously as she screwed the lid back on the peanut butter jar. When she finished chewing, she said, "Mom's friend went shopping. You can check my room to see if Oliver's lying on the bed."

Jake entered the room adorned with band posters and shelves ladened with assembled Star Wars Lego kits. As the teenager predicted, Oliver lay sprawled on top of her pajamas on her bed, his legs stretched out. He opened one eye and meowed a greeting before closing it again. Jake gathered the sleepy cat up, put him in the cage, and carried him back to the condo entrance.

Emilie scraped uneaten crusts into the garbage when Jake returned. She didn't turn to face Jake when she said, "You wouldn't like to leave Oliver here, would you? He's happy here. I'm going to miss him."

"The thought occurred to me, Em, but I promised my wife I would look after him." He laughed. "Plus, I don't suppose your mom would appreciate having a cat around. Oliver tolerates me, but I'm not sure he would do the same for your mom or vice versa."

Emilie slid the dishes into the slots in the dishwasher and turned to face Jake. "Yup, you have a point. Speaking of Mom, she left late for work this morning. She was just leaving when I got home from my friend's. She surprised me. Looked happier than I've seen her for a while. I wonder why." She glanced at Jake with a wry smile.

Jake felt his face color. *This perceptiveness must run in the family. What is it with these two?* He mustered, "I don't know, Em. She's just a cheerful person. Thanks for looking after Oliver for me. He and I both appreciate it."

Jake escaped with Oliver riding shotgun in the cage before the homicide detective's daughter asked more questions.

CHAPTER THIRTEEN

JAKE'S HOUSE WAS a reddish-brick bungalow that sat among mature trees in the well-established neighborhood. The kitchen sat at the front of the house with a large window overlooking the porch and front yard. The hardwood-covered hall ran from front to back with rooms on each side. Two bedrooms, one of which served as Jake's office, occupied the main floor, and a stairwell led to a finished basement and another bedroom. Since Mia passed, he stored anything he couldn't find space for downstairs. The rarely used living room remained spotless, save for a layer of dust accumulating on the side tables. Jake often toyed with hiring a cleaner but realized he should be able to keep the house clean since he didn't work. That thought never materialized.

He spent most of his time in the sunroom overlooking the yard at the back of the house. He passed a recent afternoon reducing the pile of magazines he planned to read someday, sitting by his chair. It was still an impressive stack. A large TV screen, of which he was fond, occupied one wall, and a drawing by Emilie replaced a gigantic clock that used to hang opposite his chair. He had decided it was time and reluctantly removed a photo of Mia from the wall. He kept a smaller version on the desk in his office. A bookshelf held his retirement plaque, assorted books, and a few of Mia's favorite knickknacks that he couldn't bring himself to discard.

The faint odor of chemicals greeted Jake when he opened the door to his home, but it smelled more like the natural scent of a house closed and uninhabited for a few days. It was that stuffy "open some windows and air me out" kind of smell. Jake released Oliver from his cage and watched him amble for his food dish. He suspected Oliver would consider it a run. "I'll fill your dish in a minute, Oliver. You'd think they starved you over there. I doubt that happened. Let me settle in, and I'll get you some food."

The gleaming floors in the hallway reflected the sunlight shining through the kitchen window. Jake knew Mia would love them. He removed his shoes, tossed his bag on the bed, and hung his jacket in the front hall cupboard. He opened windows in the kitchen, bedroom, and sunroom to ensure a cross breeze, although there wasn't a lot of air movement outside. Not wanting to heat the house with the humid outdoor air, he resolved to close the windows soon. Opening them later that night would be more beneficial, he thought, but at least now, some of the stuffiness would be removed.

He poured food for Oliver and a glass of white wine for himself, which he placed on the end table he'd moved back the last time he came to the house. From his perspective, the additional fee he paid the contractor to move furniture away from and back to its spot was priceless. Some of it just needed minor adjustments. He heaved his beloved recliner a few inches back to its spot in the sunroom before sitting down and pondering everything that happened in the last few days. The explosion, the fatalities, the old lady that nearly ran him down, Willow and the missing accountant, finding out about his baby girl's pregnancy, and last night with Dani. The night with Dani seemed so natural, and he was even better because Mia somehow told him it was okay. That she didn't want him to be alone.

Dani's divorce had been messy, and she worried about Emilie. She made it clear she didn't want to rush into anything, and Jake agreed.

But after last night, he looked forward to a closer relationship than the one they had so far.

Jake's thoughts turned to the explosion, and the people lost—young lives taken because of carelessness or a maintenance issue. An emptiness overwhelmed him when he spent too much time thinking about it, and he suspected he might suffer from survivor's guilt. He could have been in that house, but for some reason, he wasn't. He realized he shouldn't concentrate on the victims and tried to focus on what may have caused the explosion if it wasn't deliberate. Perhaps the workmen didn't install the gas line correctly in the first place, and time and wear and tear took care of the rest. That would be for the Fire Marshall to figure out.

Troubling thoughts still invaded Jake's mind, though. What happened to the accountant? Did he check out before the explosion? That was certainly possible. It would explain why he escaped the blast. But strangely, his name wasn't on the guest list at all. He didn't appear to know the owners based on the discussion around the table, so why would he have breakfast there? And where was Willow?

The guy at the hotel crept into his mind again. He just wouldn't stay out of Jake's thoughts. It may have been nothing, but Jake sensed he was being watched. The guy didn't hide it either. He seemed to be everywhere Jake was. It unnerved Jake so much he got up to peer through the front window. It wouldn't have surprised him to see a dark car on the street, but there was none.

And why did none of the residents at the B&B except Willow have a social media presence? Maybe understandable for the Thorpes since Craig worked for the military. Maybe he was Special Forces and didn't want his and his wife's identities spread across the internet. But why the Demirs? They owned and operated a Bed and Breakfast, so wouldn't they want all the publicity they could get?

Oliver strolled into the room and thumped himself down on the floor in front of Jake's chair. Jake felt sleepy, so he put the footrest up on his recliner to take a nap when his phone rang. Dani's name appeared on the screen.

"Hi, Dani, how are you?"

"I'm great, Jake. Still savoring last night and looking forward to doing it again soon. How about you?"

"Last night was amazing, Dani. Did you get enough sleep?"

"Well, as they say, I can sleep when I'm dead. When I slept, it was like I passed out. I wanted to let you know there's been a development in the case. They moved more of the rubble, and guess what? They found more remains in the furnace room in the basement. It could be Willow or the missing accountant. I won't go into the gory details, but they discovered the remains at the epicenter of the blast, so there wasn't much left. Enough to gather DNA and let the forensic people do their work to match it to somebody, though. My colleagues haven't been able to locate next of kin for anyone. Still working on it."

"Huh! Interesting that they found the body in the furnace room."

"Yes, but we're still not jumping to conclusions. There wasn't enough to identify the person as male or female. Forensics will determine the gender and hopefully identify the body, but that will take a while. This is still not officially a homicide. The remains found in the furnace room could mean that's where they landed after the blast. It could be nothing. There just isn't enough evidence. The Fire Marshall and his team arrived from Toronto and started investigating. If I had the resources, I would check into the victims' backgrounds a little further, but you know…I don't. The other thing I wanted to tell you is that my colleagues finished running down the license plates and are matching them to the victims. The last I heard there were fewer cars than victims. I have to run, Jake. I'll keep you posted, okay?"

"Yes, of course, Dani. Thanks for letting me know."

Jake pressed the key to end the call. Any thoughts of sleep had vanished. He pushed the lever on the chair to put the footrest down and rose to walk into his bedroom. Both he and Dani knew her comment about lack of resources to investigate the deceased further would be like a dog whistle to him, and he was about to answer the call. A large whiteboard hung on the wall inside the entrance to his office and to the right of his desk. He switched on the light and retrieved a blue dry erase pen and an eraser from his desk drawer. He erased the "to-do" list he wrote as a reminder of the preparations needed for the floor replacement.

Once he cleaned the board, he retrieved the sheet he wrote on at the hotel and transcribed the information across the top. He added one additional entry. "Unknown" to represent the man who watched him.

Underneath each name, he wrote the questions swirling like a whirlpool in his mind. He smiled a crooked smile, knowing he would do this anyway, even without Dani's prompt. As an entry at the bottom, he wrote, "Why would someone kill a bunch of people to get at one?" If this became a homicide investigation, that would become the pressing question. And one that he wanted to find the answer to.

CHAPTER FOURTEEN

JAKE TOSSED AND turned during the night, alternating between wrapping the covers around himself and throwing them off, brooding about the questions surrounding the explosion. Dani thought the explosion was accidental, but he uncovered too much uncertainty to suit him. When he rolled over for what seemed like the 37th time and tried to find a comfortable spot for his head on his misshapen pillow, he realized he needed to plunge into his own investigation until the fire investigator proved conclusively the blast was an accident. Either that or try to forget about it altogether. The second option was not in his DNA. He needed answers for himself and to honor the victims.

The bedside clock ticked to six o'clock when he opened his bleary eyes to see Oliver curled up, sound asleep at the end of the bed on the side that used to be occupied by Mia. He chose the spot as his favorite since Mia rescued him from the pound. Jake wondered whether Oliver would welcome Dani if it came to that.

Jake climbed out of bed and pulled on navy blue sweatpants and a black tee shirt. Oliver stretched on the bed before thumping to the floor and wandering to the kitchen. Jake fed the cat, brewed coffee, and toasted two slices of rye toast that he slathered with peanut butter. He and Dani's daughter connected on a few levels, and one commonality was their love of toast and peanut butter. The cat finished his meal and settled onto his perch in front of the kitchen window where he observed the never-ending battle between an obnoxious blue jay and a determined squirrel over the seed in the bird feeder. By the way he settled in, Oliver seemed comfortable on his observation post as Jake carried the plate and toast into the office and sat in his leather chair to ponder the questions on the whiteboard.

Who were these people with no social media presence?

Jake accepted the earlier premise that the Thorpes could have a valid reason for avoiding the internet since Craig worked in the military. Willow would be the logical place to start, but there was no confirmation that she was a victim, so it would be a tough conversation to have with her social media friends. He focused on people who reviewed the B&B on their website. He searched for the B&B site and noted that one person, a Lucy Pottinger, stated in her review she stayed several times. She might know the Demirs, Jake decided.

Her review stated she lived in Peterborough, Ontario, about three hours from Ottawa. Jake tried a phone lookup site that Avery showed him on the internet, and it surprised him when a phone number popped up for Ms. Pottinger. She must be one of the few remaining people with a landline, Jake thought.

He dialed the number, and a woman answered. She sounded elderly, although Jake knew from his experience with telephone interviews during his reporting years that it was often impossible to tell. When she confirmed she was Lucy Pottinger, Jake said, "I'm a reporter for the Ottawa newspaper." A little white lie never hurt when he questioned someone. He used another tactic from his reporter days, continuing before the woman could ask questions. He assumed the woman had heard about the explosion since it had been all over the news. "I learned from reviews on the Sweet Dreams' website that you stayed there several times."

"Yes, it's my favorite place to stay when I'm in Ottawa. My daughter lives in the city in a condo with my grandkids. What is this about?"

Jake's mind flashed to his impending grandfather status as he realized he might have jumped to a conclusion.

"Oh, I'm sorry, I thought you might know. I'm sorry to tell you this, but there was an explosion at the Sweet Dreams, and the owners, along with a few others who stayed there, lost their lives. It's been in the news. I hoped you might provide a few details about the people that owned the place."

Lucy's voice faltered. It became apparent to Jake from her reaction that she had some connection with the owners. "That's horrible. No, I didn't know. I stopped listening to the news and canceled my newspaper. I focus on the local news; sometimes, it's not that positive either. There's too much death and destruction in the world, and nobody ever reports the good things."

"That's why I called you, Ms. Pottinger. I want to write an article about the owners. They deserve to be heard."

Jake winced and reminded himself to suggest to his friend, Janice, at the newspaper to contact Ms. Pottinger for a background article on the Demirs. He had no control over what Janice reported, but he thought it might be interesting to readers and would salve his conscience about his lie.

The line went quiet. Then, he heard the woman blow her nose.

"Ms. Pottinger, are you alright?"

She came back on the line and sniffed. "Yes, I just had to compose myself. That's dreadful news. Call me Lucy, please. I got to know Omar and Seda during the many times I stayed there. They were so gracious when I first met them, and I just had to go back. They were considerate and friendly. Running a B&B was the perfect job for them, in my opinion. They made their guests comfortable. Not only did they provide a substantial breakfast, but if they had time, they would have tea with their tenants in the evening. Omar always joked and pointed out things people could do around town. That's why I kept going back. They always welcomed me."

"Are you familiar with their background?"

"They both came to Canada from Turkey quite a few years ago.

They met at university. I don't know which one. They didn't have any kids. Omar always fussed about at the B&B, either inside or in the yard, but someone came in to do the housekeeping. I knew Omar better than Seda. I think Seda worked at something else besides the Bed and Breakfast. She helped with the breakfast preparation, but she didn't seem to be around during the day."

"Did they ever have trouble with any of their guests that you're aware of?"

"Oh no, just the opposite. Everybody I talked to loved them. Why would you ask that? The explosion was an accident, wasn't it? A gas explosion of some kind?"

"There's no reason to believe otherwise right now, Lucy. I'm just covering all the bases."

"Well, you make sure you say nice things about them. They were a delightful couple and deserve to be remembered that way. You don't happen to know when the funeral will be, do you? I would drive up to pay my last respects. That's how much I thought of them." She hesitated for an instant. "Oh, dear, I'll need to find somewhere else to stay. I loved it so much there. It's so sad."

"I haven't heard yet about the funeral, but I'm sure an announcement will be in the obituaries. I will certainly include everything you've told me in the article, Lucy."

They spent the next few minutes talking about Omar and Seda, but Lucy added little else. When they hung up, Jake tried to contact other guests who left reviews. He touched base with two, both of whom heard about the explosion. One was more forthcoming than the other, but the consensus was that the Demirs were a lovely couple, and there would be no reason for anyone to want to harm them.

CHAPTER FIFTEEN

AS JAKE ROSE to add to his notes on the whiteboard, he glanced at his watch and saw it was noon already. Only then did he realize how hungry he was. He grabbed the dry erase marker and added, "Everyone loved Omar, but no one really knew Seda" to his notes before sauntering to the kitchen. He found Oliver sprawled on his perch, sound asleep. The cat twitched when Jake entered the room, making him believe Oliver was dreaming about having the blue jay, squirrel, or both for a noon snack.

As Jake prepared a grilled cheese sandwich for himself, his phone rang. It was Dani. The two exchanged pleasantries before Dani got to the point of her call.

"The coroner established it was Willow Altman's remains in the furnace room. Her next of kin are being notified. I also spoke to one investigator from the Office of the Fire Marshall. He told me they first investigated whether the explosion originated from the outside and burned in or from the inside out. It was clear from the blast pattern that the fire originated inside the building. Their next step was to investigate the point of origin. When I said the furnace room was ground zero, I wasn't totally correct. The devastation was so great they haven't been able to determine the origin point for the explosion, other than to say it started in the house. They're still investigating."

"I'm sorry to hear about the young lady. She had the rest of her life in front of her."

"Yes, all I know is that she was in her twenties and worked as an Executive Assistant to a Member of Parliament until recently. She had a degree in public administration, so she had a future. I have no idea what happened with her job, but maybe if you have nothing else to do, you could find out." She chuckled. "I might have to put you on the payroll."

Jake chuckled along with Dani. "What else would I be doing if I wasn't sticking my nose into investigations?"

They continued to chat for a few minutes before hanging up. Jake walked back to his office, sat in his chair, and crunched on one of the dill pickles he always had with his grilled cheese sandwich. *What was it they said on the cooking shows? Oh yes, it elevated his grilled cheese.* As he chewed, he thought about what he'd just heard. He continued eating his sandwich with his left hand while he controlled the mouse with his right. As he discovered before, Willow Altman's social media sites revealed a treasure trove of contacts. Willow identified her hometown as Ottawa, so it seemed strange to Jake that she would stay at a B&B. Then he remembered his own situation, having to leave his house because of construction. Maybe she was moving and hadn't updated her profile, he thought. There was no mention of a place of work.

Jake finished his sandwich and wiped his mouth with a napkin. He consulted his notes from the hotel and verified one "friend" on social media who seemed to pop up more than the others. Her name was Julie Tremblay. Jake called her. She answered on the third ring.

"Hi, Julie. My name is Jake Scott. I'm a reporter with the newspaper here in Ottawa. I noticed your name on Willow Altman's social media and wondered if I could ask a few questions about her."

"A reporter? What? Have you heard from Willow? I don't understand."

"Yes, I'm a reporter, and we're doing a piece on the explosion in Westboro. I…"

"The explosion? Is that where Willow was? Is she okay? I've been trying to reach her since last week. Tell me she's okay."

"I'm sorry to tell you this, Julie, but Willow was staying at the Sweet Dreams Bed and Breakfast. She was there during the explosion, and she didn't make it."

A gasp came from the other end of the line. Then, "Oh, my God. He did it. He actually did it. I warned her a long time ago, but she wouldn't listen. She became infatuated with the man. I always thought he was dangerous. She was probably staying at a B&B to hide from that asshole." She blurted the words out in one long sentence, but she sounded to Jake like she was more angry than sad.

Jake tried to slow her down. "Listen, Julie, do you have time to talk now? Or I can meet you someplace."

"Yes, I want to hear more about what happened. Willow and I didn't socialize much. We were more working and social media friends than actual friends. She was younger than me. I felt sorry for her in some ways. She was gorgeous and smart. She could have done better. I can meet you after work. Around five o'clock. I live in Orleans, but I could meet you downtown as long as I can be at the stop before the last bus leaves at 6:20. What did you say your name was again?"

"Jake Scott. Is there a coffee shop near your work where I could meet you?"

"How about the Bridgehead on Sparks Street? I'll be wearing a blue dress and carrying a briefcase."

"That works for me, Julie. Thank you very much. I'll see you at 5:00."

When they hung up, Jake wondered who the "he" was that Julie alluded to. It sounded like Julie thought "he" was capable of murder. *Could Willow Altman be the reason for the explosion? Could someone want to get rid of her so bad they would kill several other people to do so?*

It seemed like a stretch to Jake, but he had lived long enough, seen enough, and reported on enough that he believed people could do almost anything.

CHAPTER SIXTEEN

THE DRIVE DOWNTOWN from Westboro only took a few minutes despite the rush hour traffic. People working from home since the pandemic made commuting easier for those who did drive, although construction was always a nightmare in the summer. Ottawa residents considered construction to be the season following winter. Jake also noticed an uptick in aggressive drivers since the pandemic. However, taking all that into account and parking in the World Exchange Plaza put him at the Bridgehead coffee shop on Sparks Street at ten minutes to five. He glanced at the menu of mind-boggling choices on the wall, but always the traditionalist, he ordered a medium-brewed coffee.

A woman appearing to be in her late twenties, wearing a blue sundress and carrying a briefcase, walked through the door twenty minutes later. She wore curly brown hair to her shoulders and large round sunglasses perched on top of her head. Jake recognized her the minute she walked in from her profile picture on social media, so he rose from his chair and raised his hand to attract her attention. They shook hands, and he asked if he could get her something. She thanked him and asked for a chai latte, and something called a peanut butter chocolate energy bite. Jake repeated the order to himself to remember it as he approached the counter.

He decided the energy bite looked appealing, so he purchased one for himself, carried the order back to the table, handed it to the young woman, and sat facing her.

"Thank you for agreeing to meet me, Julie. I appreciate it. I'm sorry to have to break the news to you about Willow. My understanding is that you worked together?"

"We both worked as executive assistants to Members of Parliament. We attended meetings together, so we got to know each other. Sometimes, we would go on coffee breaks together, walk behind the Parliament Buildings at lunchtime, or shop on Sparks Street. We got to know each other some. What happened at the Bed and Breakfast?"

Jake blew on his coffee to cool it before taking a sip as he listened. He nibbled on his bite and wiped his mouth. He wanted the woman's confidence and didn't want to scare her off, so he trod lightly.

"My understanding is the police are still investigating. I'm hoping to do a backgrounder on the people who stayed at the B&B. They deserve to have their stories told so readers know we lost some good people. I would appreciate any help you can give me." He removed his phone from his pocket. "Is it okay if I record your thoughts?"

Jake observed tears forming in the corners of Julie's eyes as she nodded in the affirmative. She said, "Willow was intelligent, and I envisioned her with a brilliant future. She was funny and fun to be around. A hard worker. It's a demanding job working for a Member of Parliament. The hours are long. We spend a lot of time with our bosses. We travel with them. Sometimes things happen."

Jake saw where this was going. He let Julie talk.

The woman looked around to see who was nearby before continuing. "Willow worked for an MP from Saskatchewan who was in his forties. He was tall, good looking, and worked on Parliament Hill for some time. Willow loved working for him, but we all heard rumors about the guy. We all knew he had trouble keeping his hands to himself, and we stayed away from him, but Willow thought he was special, that he was the one for her. We also heard rumors he could get violent. To my knowledge, the police never charged him with anything, maybe because of who he was. He was in a position of power. He could destroy anyone's career if he wanted to, so nobody wanted to talk about what he was really like.

"I've worked for eight years in various roles on the Hill, so I've heard more of the scuttlebutt than Willow. She only worked there for about three years. Most of what you hear isn't true, of course. People like to sensationalize things and pretend they know more than they do to be popular, but the stories about this MP were so commonplace that there had to be something to them."

Julie took a bite of her cookie and washed it down with her latte. She kept her eyes on her plate, picking at her napkin, hesitating as if wondering how much more she should say. She brushed a crumb from her cheek with her thumb. Finally, she said, "I've said too much. Are you going to print this? The MP will get me fired if he finds out it was me who talked about him…or worse." She shuffled in her seat, obviously uncomfortable, as she raised her heavy-lidded eyes to meet Jake's.

Jake said, "Julie, thank you for being so frank with me. I'm going to be completely honest with you to make sure you understand what I'm doing. I no longer work for the newspaper. I'm retired, but I have a friend who works for Ottawa Police Service, and I'm doing some preliminary investigating for her to determine if there might have been foul play."

Julie's face turned pale in front of Jake's eyes. She grimaced as if about to be sick. Jake continued. "If there's any reason at all to believe the Member of Parliament could be involved in some plot to kill Willow, you need to tell me. I lied to you at the beginning. I won't be publishing anything. My former colleague at the paper might want some background on Willow, but I'm more interested in why the explosion could have happened. It still might be an accident, but if not, we need to know for the sake of the people who were in the blast. You've been a great help so far, but I think there's more. Help us, Julie."

Julie pursed her lips and fought back the tears.

"Okay... I'll tell you what I think, but please keep my name out of it. I'm a single mom, and I need this job."

Jake nodded. "I'll need to tell my friend at the police department, but that's as far as it will go."

Julie waited a few beats and then added to her story.

"Willow told me she planned to see this MP after working hours. His name is Dan Rivera. He's not in a ministerial position, but he's still powerful. Maybe not as powerful as he pictures himself, but he has the power to ruin lives. I don't know if he would go to the extent of having someone killed, though. Willow told me things became so serious that Rivera told her he would leave his wife. I didn't believe it, so I told Willow that. There had been similar rumors about other people before. I told Willow about the stories of Rivera becoming violent, but she ignored me. She became upset with me, and we didn't speak for a while.

"Last week, Willow told me she found out he was dating someone else all the time he saw her. Willow was furious but scared, I guess because of what I told her. We went for coffee in this very location, and she was a mess. She couldn't stop crying. I understood her being upset because she was determined to break up with him, but it seemed to be over the top."

Jake slumped back in his chair. He sensed more yet to the story. He watched Julie draw in a deep breath before continuing.

She said, "I asked her what she was going to do, and she said she planned to confront him and tell his wife what a jerk he was. I warned her it could cost her job, but she had principles and said it would be worth it to make sure he didn't hurt any other women. She confessed to me she had seen his temper and feared for her safety when they were seeing each other, so she worried about his reaction. When I asked what she would do to protect herself, she said she would find a place to stay. She didn't tell me where. I guess it was the Bed and Breakfast." Julie stopped speaking and used the napkin to wipe her eyes. She scrunched the napkin into a ball and dropped it on the table.

Jake leaned forward to put his hand on Julie's shoulder. He said, "Thank you for being so honest with me, Julie. I can't tell you how much I appreciate this."

Julie sniffed. Her face crumpled, the corners of her mouth turned down, and her eyes were moist with tears. She said, "I…I should have warned her sooner…been more…I don't know…persistent. I feel responsible, but it was too late when she told me she was going to confront him." Her bottom lip trembled. "There was no stopping her because there was another thing that I haven't mentioned. Things went too far."

Julie dabbed at her eyes with a tissue as she seemed to summon the courage to finish her story.

"She was pregnant."

The revelation sent a shockwave vibrating through Jake when she spoke the words, although he prepared himself for this. He had a feeling leading up to this point. His thoughts flashed to his daughter. About how happy she sounded. And how sad it must have made Willow when her dreams dissolved. No wonder she seemed so downcast at the breakfast table. He had one more question. "Do you know when Willow planned to tell Rivera that she was pregnant and ending the relationship?"

"Yes," she answered sadly. "The day of the explosion."

CHAPTER SEVENTEEN

JAKE AND JULIE finished their snacks and coffee and chatted for a few more minutes until he sensed that the conversation had gone as far as it would go. He shut off his phone recorder and thanked Julie for being so forthright. He asked if he could drive her somewhere. She glanced at her watch and decided she had time to make her stop before her bus arrived.

"Even if it's to Orleans. I don't mind driving you to the east end, Julie. You've been incredibly honest. Seriously, I don't mind giving you a lift. I have nowhere I need to be."

Julie replied in a subdued voice, "Thank you, Jake. I'd like to use the time on the bus to compose myself. This has been incredibly tiring. Hearing about Willow's death and then realizing I could have or should have done more has worn me down. It's a special time I spend with my kids in the evenings before they go to bed, and I don't want to be a mess when I get there. The bus ride will give me a chance to pull it together. Just promise me, if Rivera had anything to do with Willow's death, you'll crucify that son of a bitch."

"You were a very special friend to Willow, Julie. You warned her. People have to want to be helped, and it sounds like you did everything possible. I promise you I'll pass along everything you've told me to my friend in the Homicide division. If this turns out to be anything more than a horrible accident, I know her well enough that I can tell you she will dig into it and deal with anyone responsible."

He left Julie sitting at the table fixing her makeup to repair the damage her tears caused and headed out in the sultry evening to retrieve his car at the World Exchange Plaza. His stomach growled on the way to the parking lot, suggesting he needed something more substantial than the delicacy he just finished. A drink stronger than coffee wouldn't hurt either. He regretted not ordering a wrap at the coffee house.

Restocking his groceries was one thing he planned to do that had yet to be done. It would have to be done on the way home, and the thought of waiting to eat before grocery shopping wasn't appealing. *What was it they said about grocery shopping when you're hungry? Oh yes, don't do it.*

He made an abrupt U-turn toward a favorite neighborhood restaurant he had frequented occasionally during his working days, D'Arcy McGee's Irish Pub on Sparks Street. As he approached, the hubbub and laughter from the restaurant rose above the sound of the people walking and talking on Sparks. The lively evening crowd occupied many of the seats in the L-shaped outdoor patio next to two sides of the building. Jake spied two empty tables and made a beeline for one of them. He sat under a large eight-sided black umbrella with "Guinness" emblazoned in large white lettering on the edges of each panel. The female server arrived at his table right away with a bubbly, friendly, and efficient manner in tow. Shepherd's pie tempted him, but he always considered it comfort food for a rainy or snowy day, so he opted for the house favorite of fish and chips. The not-so-subtle Guinness advertising on the umbrellas convinced him to order a large glass of the velvety smooth coffee and chocolate-flavored Irish stout.

Jake had little time to contemplate everything Julie told him before the server brought his Guinness. He thought of contacting Dani, but he could barely hear himself think as the energetic crowd tried to outdo each other, making a phone conversation next to impossible. He wondered what she was doing. The Market where the knifing she was working on took place was about a ten-minute walk from where he sat. He would wait to call her until he got home. His meal arrived, and he began to enjoy his fish and chips while scanning the crowd on the off chance he might recognize someone. Ottawa was just small enough that it happened more often than one would expect.

He was about half finished with the large piece of golden beer-battered haddock and half paying attention when someone he thought he knew walked by. Well, he didn't *know* him, but he had met him. He closed and re-opened his eyes and shook his head. *Could his eyes be deceiving him?* Jake only caught a fleeting glimpse of the man's face as he passed by. Now as Jake stared at the man's back, there was a familiarity to the way he walked. Hunched shoulders like a painful back bothered him. The man who stomped away from the breakfast table at the Bed and Breakfast walked the same way. Jake was sure the man was the accountant.

Jake scraped his chair back on the brick patio and leaped from the table, pulling his napkin from his belt as he rose. He remembered he hadn't paid, so he frantically sought the server. He glanced at the man disappearing down the street as he flagged the server down. Rushing over to her, he said, "I just saw someone I think I know walking down the street. I promise I'm not trying to run out without paying." He fished in his pocket for his wallet and extracted his credit card. "Here. Here's my card. I'll be back in a minute."

She took the card and stammered something as Jake raced through the entrance to the patio with the eyes of every patron on his back. He couldn't see the man he believed to be the accountant. Dammit, this can't be happening, he thought. The man had disappeared. Jake scanned the area and asked himself where the man could have gone. He wasn't walking that quickly, so he must have disappeared into one of the neighboring buildings. Or maybe he parked his car in a nearby garage. The only nearby parking that he knew of was at the National Arts Centre or City Hall, which were both in the opposite direction, or at the World Exchange Plaza where he parked. Jake ran to the corner of

Sparks Street and Metcalfe to look down the street, but the man wasn't walking toward the Plaza.

Jake walked slowly past the buildings on Sparks, looking for a sign suggesting that an accountant was occupying the space inside. He even tugged on the doors to the buildings, opening the ones he could to peer at the business names in the lobbies. Many of the owners had locked up because of the lateness of the evening. Security guards stared at him as he rattled the door on two buildings, but they didn't budge from their seats. The names on plaques he could see through the window included lawyers and other businesses but no accountants. Then he realized the accountant may not own a practice. He could work as the chief financial officer for a business.

Jake finally decided he was wasting his time. He could have been mistaken, anyway. Maybe it wasn't the accountant. He thought Dani was right. Everything that happened to him could have had a greater effect than he realized. Perhaps he was letting things bother him that amounted to nothing. But now he could add something else to the list of things bothering him as he turned glumly back toward the restaurant. Something about the business names he saw.

The woman with the bubbly personality who had served him now looked impatient and harried as she dealt with a lineup of customers waiting for a table. Some gestured toward his empty chair beside a table with a used napkin, a plate of half-eaten fish and chips, and a half-full glass of Guinness. He caught the server's eye and sheepishly asked for a takeout box for his fish and chips, took two deep swallows of the Guinness, wiped his mouth with the napkin, and settled his bill with an extra large tip.

CHAPTER EIGHTEEN

JAKE TRIED TO get his head around the day's events as he drove home. Julie's comments about Willow were eye-opening and certainly provocative. Her revelations about the Member of Parliament made him wonder if the politician could have been angry enough at Willow and so worried about his career and marriage that he would blow up an entire house full of people to keep his secret. It was possible, but plausible? Jake reflected on some people he had interviewed over the years, knowing there was no end to the depravity of some people as sad as that was to acknowledge.

Then, there was the sighting of the person he believed to be the accountant. He was certain he wasn't seeing things, even though the man disappeared like a puff of smoke in the evening breeze. Jake didn't want his imagination to carry him away. He knew he had to be logical and proceed accordingly.

He arrived at his house and parked in the garage, not remembering the drive home. It was like the car was on autopilot and knew the way by itself. It happened many times before when he worked, and his thoughts took over. The one thing he remembered was that he still hadn't gone grocery shopping.

When he entered the house, Oliver was nowhere to be seen. He found the cat asleep in his favorite spot at the end of the bed. Jake often wondered if the cat spent his waking hours when he was away looking for Mia, especially since Oliver was just home after spending time at Dani's place. Maybe he had forgotten Mia hadn't been around for over two years.

Jake ensured Oliver had enough to eat and drink and warmed up the rest of his fish and chips in the microwave. He tossed a chip in his mouth on the way to the sunroom and grimaced. French fries never tasted the same warmed up. Maybe there was a trick to reheating French fries he wasn't aware of. As he sat in his recliner, he decided it was a question he would have to pose to Dani.

And that's exactly who he called when he finished his meal. She sounded chipper when she answered, "Hey, handsome, how's it goin'"?

"It's going just fine, thank you, sweetie. What're you up to?"

"Emilie and I are watching a romcom on TV and hanging out in our pajamas. I grabbed the remote before her, or we'd be watching a horror flick. It's been a long time since we've done this. What's new with you?"

"Oh, I don't want to keep you from your movie. Call me when you get a minute."

"It's okay. The movie's on pause, and Emilie's microwaving popcorn. You'll soon be able to hear it." She chuckled. "How has your day been?"

Clearly, she wanted to hear if he had made any progress, so he relayed the conversation with Julie. He pictured where Dani and Emilie sat on the sofa in the living room from the sound of the microwave door slamming shut in the background, followed by slow popping that built to a fever pitch before it stopped altogether. The microwave door slammed shut again, and strangely, Jake could almost smell the hot buttered popcorn from blocks away. That brought him to thoughts of the power of suggestion as images of the man he thought was the accountant filled his head. He hadn't told Dani about that yet.

After a few seconds of silence, Dani said, "It sounds like Mr. Rivera might be desperate to cover his tracks, but enough to commit a multiple homicide? How would he know where Willow went unless he followed her? Why not just run her down or something? Sorry, but it doesn't seem likely, Jake."

"I agree there are still a lot of questions. I'm going to talk to Rivera to get a better grasp of the type of person he is." Jake hesitated for a moment, wondering if Dani would think he was crazy with what he was about to say.

"There's one other thing if you have time."

"Sure, Emilie will have eaten all the popcorn by the time I get off the phone, but I've gained a few pounds, so you might do me a favor. What is it?"

"I think I saw the accountant downtown."

"Interesting. You *think* you did, or you did?"

"I think I did." Jake told Dani how he had glimpsed the man he thought was the accountant and tried to follow him with no luck. He waited to see if Dani thought he was losing it completely.

Dani said, "I know you won't let this go, Jake. What are you going to do? If you promise to keep me in the loop, I'll go along with whatever you decide."

"I need to go downtown during the day to see if I can spot him again. I'll do that tomorrow. Something bothered me when I checked the business names on the buildings, but I can't put my finger on it. I want to look again to figure out what it was. It's been nagging me like a mosquito that won't go away during the night, and I need to find out why."

"I had one of those a couple of nights ago. Mosquito, that is. If I could have seen it, I might have shot it. I let it sting me so I could smash it. That's the way I dealt with it. Do what you must do, Jake. Just keep me posted. Now, this movie has a young lady in a small town who's about to lose the man of her dreams to a job in the big city. Emilie and I have to watch her solve her problems. If she can, of course, right, Em? My daughter just rolled her eyes, but she said to say hi. Take care and call me tomorrow, Jake."

Jake confirmed he would and spent the rest of the evening researching a Member of Parliament named Dan Rivera.

CHAPTER NINETEEN

JAKE SLEPT FITFULLY again throughout the night. Whatever nagged at him wouldn't let go, so he woke countless times trying to pinpoint the reason. Nothing came to him. Around four a.m., he convinced himself only another tour of the buildings that caused his mind to go into overdrive would solve the problem, and he fell asleep, only to wake at seven.

Although never energetic, Oliver seemed extra lethargic in the morning, too. He ambled after Jake to his dish and munched on his food. It differed from most days when the cat couldn't devour his meal fast enough. Jake wondered if Oliver didn't feel well or was just imitating his own listless demeanor.

Jake puttered in the kitchen, cleaning up and putting things away. He tried to find a place for everything instead of leaving dishes in the dishwasher or on the table or hiding them in the oven. He smiled at Dani's influence on him. While his house would never win a good housekeeping award, it was better than before Dani came into the picture. He never knew when she might show up, so he attempted to maintain a semblance of order, occasionally even dusting the end table in the living room.

After showering and dressing in khaki shorts and a blue short-sleeved shirt, which he left untucked, he poured another coffee and wandered into his office. He set the coffee on a coaster on his desk and sat in his chair, while glancing at a number he scribbled on a notepad the night before. The number belonged to the office of Dan Rivera. The website Jake researched revealed much about Dan Rivera's work but little else. His profile pic showed a distinguished man with a generous smile and dark hair with gray streaks. His wide smile made his eyes close in a squint. He wore a blue suit with a paler blue patterned tie. Jake understood the attraction of the ladies.

Rivera seemed to work hard at his job. He belonged to several committees, and the site listed multiple interventions in parliamentary discussions. Rivera's expenditures revealed he spent $28,000 on travel and over $40,000 on contract work. Jake didn't know offhand whether the expenditures were in line with other parliamentarians. It would be something to investigate.

Jake dialed the number for Rivera's office. A young-sounding woman answered. "Mr. Rivera's office. How can I help you?" Visions of a despondent Willow Altman sitting at the breakfast table at the B&B flooded Jake's brain.

"Good morning," Jake said. "I'm a reporter for an Ottawa newspaper. Could I please speak to Mr. Rivera about a personal matter?"

"I'm sorry, but Mr. Rivera has meetings all day. Perhaps I can help you?"

"No, I don't think so. As I said, it's a personal matter. Maybe you could pass along a message for me. Just tell him I'm a reporter, and I would like to ask him a few questions about Willow Altman. Tell him I have some information from several sources regarding his relationship with Ms. Altman that I'll be running in tomorrow's newspaper, and I would like to give him a chance to comment." Jake recited his phone number.

It was like the silence sucked the air from the room while the woman at the other end of the line apparently considered what to say next. Finally, when she came back on the line, all pretense of the perky, willing-to-help assistant disappeared. She said in an even tone, "Can I have your name again, please?"

"Jake Scott."

"Okay, thank you. I'll pass the message along."

She hung up.

Jake snickered to himself. From his experience reporting on other politicians, he knew they didn't like to be embarrassed in the news. He expected a return call any minute.

It took longer than expected, but the call came. "Unknown number" appeared on the screen.

The voice sounded demanding. Angry. "Jake Scott?"

"Yes, this is Jake Scott." He asked innocently, "With whom am I speaking?"

"You know damn well who this is, Scott. And I know you're a *former* reporter. You lied to my assistant. I remember you from when you *were* a reporter, though. Always trying to dig up dirt on hard-working people. I have precious little time for people like you, so you better be quick. What do you want?"

"I think you know I only reported facts in my day, Mr. Rivera. Or may I call you Dan? It would be much simpler. You're right, I lied to your assistant, but I wanted to make sure you got the message. I still have friends at the paper. Depending on our conversation, I may or may not pass my information on to them to investigate, so let's get off on the right foot and be honest with each other. I'll get right to the point. Did you have anything to do with the explosion at the Sweet Dreams Bed and Breakfast?"

"What!? That's preposterous. Why would I have something to do with such a tragedy? The implication is disgusting. I'm hanging up now."

Jake blurted. "You know your former executive assistant was in that explosion, right Dan? How do you feel about that?"

"Of course, I know. It's terrible, and we're all grieving here at the office. I feel horrible for her family."

"Is it true that Willow Altman was pregnant with your baby, Dan?"

Jake could swear he heard a gulp on the other end of the line, but Rivera kept up the indignant act.

"I don't know what the hell you're talking about, Scott. If this gets into the newspaper, I'll sue you and the paper into oblivion."

Oliver moseyed into the office and thumped down on the carpet at Jake's feet. He lay on his side, grooming himself with his paw. Jake watched the cat, grateful that he seemed to be okay, as he continued the conversation. "Well, Dan, it wouldn't do much good since I don't work for the paper anymore, remember? I don't think you would have returned my call if you didn't have some connection beyond a professional relationship with Willow Altman. Is it true you've had affairs with several women on Parliament Hill? Or at least tried to? What about the young lady I just spoke with? Is she another of your conquests?"

Jake pictured the man's red face as he blustered, "I'm a married man, Scott. These accusations have gone too far. There's no substance to anything you're saying, as usual."

"From what I've heard, you've been a naughty man, Dan. I noticed you didn't deny that you had several affairs. There is enough information from reliable sources about you and Willow Altman that I can take to my colleagues at the paper. I suspect you would have trouble getting elected president of your former high school after they print the details of your illustrious career. Your extra-curricular activities will disappoint a lot of constituents in your riding in Saskatchewan, Dan, don't you think? Good luck to you."

Jake knew this could go either way. Rivera would want to talk, or he was just the victim of vicious rumors and would hang up. He waited in the silence of his office for several seconds with his thumb hovering over the "end call" button.

CHAPTER TWENTY

DAN RIVERA DID not hang up. Instead, Jake heard him clear his throat as a door closed. Jake leaned forward to pet Oliver as Rivera came back on the phone. His voice sounded husky.

"You still there, Scott?"

"Yes, I'm here."

"I'm going to talk to you because, despite what I said earlier, I believe you were an honest reporter in your day. There's no need to go to the press with any of this. Do we have an understanding?"

"I can't promise anything about not going to the paper." He left out that he would probably take the story to the police instead. "It all depends on what you tell me. I'm prepared to listen to your side of the story. I'm trying to find out if the explosion was a terrible accident or a homicide. I'm investigating on behalf of a friend at the police department. The more people I can eliminate as possible suspects, the easier it will be for my friend if a proper investigation is required. It will be better for you if you can provide details to satisfy the investigators that you weren't involved somehow. They won't even look at you."

Rivera sighed. "Look, it's true. Willow and I dated. We spend a lot of time together doing this type of work, and one thing led to another.

Whatever reputation you envision I have with women is untrue, but Willow and I had a relationship. I was going to call it off, but I never got the chance. The explosion happened before I told her. I did tell her I found her a job with another Member of Parliament in a different area of the building so we wouldn't have to interact on a business level. I…"

"Let me stop you there, Dan. I stayed at the Bed and Breakfast the night before the explosion and had breakfast with Willow and others the morning of the blast. She was despondent and said she was unemployed."

"Yeah, I told her about the new job, and she freaked out. She told me to stick the job, threw an armful of papers at me, and stormed out of the office. That would have been the day before the explosion."

"So, why did she need to stay at a Bed and Breakfast? Wouldn't she have been more comfortable in her home?"

"I don't know. I tried to reach her all day the day of the explosion, but she wouldn't pick up. It shocked me to learn she was in the building that blew up."

"Someone told me you have violent tendencies, Dan. That she was afraid you would do something rash."

"I don't know where you heard that. It's rubbish." Indignant again.

"Okay, what about the rumor about Willow being pregnant? Any truth to that?"

Hesitation. Another deep sigh. Then finally, "Yes, she was. I offered to pay for an abortion, but she refused."

"Isn't that reason enough to cause an explosion at the Bed and Breakfast? You're not doing much to help yourself, Dan."

"I know it looks bad, but there's one thing that might help." Rivera waited for Jake to say something.

"Okay, I'm listening. What is it?"

"The baby wasn't mine. I can't have children. A doctor took care of that."

Jake sat in stunned silence as Rivera revealed how he had had a vasectomy after he and his wife had their second child. He was worried word would get out about his affair with Willow and that the media would sensationalize the story to the extent the court of public opinion would assume him to be a deadbeat dad. Fear of losing his family and job prompted him to offer to pay for the abortion to keep everything quiet. He recounted offering Willow the job in a different department and the abortion option on the same day, and that's what caused her to storm out of the office.

When Jake decided he had most of the information he was going to get, he asked one more question. "Do you know who the father was?"

"No, I asked the same question. She told me it was a drunken one-night stand. That's all she would say."

"Okay, thanks, Dan. I appreciate your honesty. I'll relay all this information to my friend at the police department."

Jake's next call was to Dani. He explained the details of his phone call to Dan Rivera.

She said, "Well, if the explosion turns out to be a homicide, I guess we have another suspect, so far name unknown. The baby's father. That was big of Rivera to offer to pay for an abortion. I guess it's his way of atoning for his sins. Was he believable?"

"I expect he was being honest with the part he told me, Dani. If he was lying, he put on a virtuoso performance. He didn't seem all that distraught about her death, though. It was more like a problem eliminated for him. He either denied parts or left them out altogether. Remember Willow's friend, Julie Tremblay, saying that Rivera had violent tendencies? Of course, he denied that. But why else would Willow leave her residence to stay at a B&B for the night? Julie also told me he's a womanizer, but he denied that, too. I wouldn't rule him out. I'll talk to Willow's friend Julie again to see if she has any thoughts on the one-night-stand guy. She really wanted to help Willow."

"It sounds like Rivera was using her."

"There's no doubt about that, Dani. Him and another person, by the sound of it. How's your case going, by the way? Any progress?"

"We're narrowing it down. Talking to suspects. Eliminating people. It's just a matter of time. How're you and Oliver doing?"

"Oliver seemed under the weather this morning, but I think he was just copying my lethargy. I didn't sleep well last night. Something still bothered me from walking past the buildings on Sparks Street yesterday. As soon as I get off the phone with you, I'll go back downtown and wander around to see if I can determine what."

"I'm sure you'll figure it out. You never really told me about the Bed and Breakfast. I love Bed and Breakfasts. We must go to one sometime. What was it like?"

"No, I guess I didn't. They decorated the room with vintage furniture. Four-poster bed. Patterned wallpaper. Old washstand with a white basin and jug. Fancy rugs everywhere throughout the house. The bathroom was something else, though. Very modern, with one of those glass shower enclosures you can see through. I guess I grew up in a different time. Not much privacy. None, in fact."

A throaty chuckle came over the phone. "I grew up around the same time as you, Jake, and I picture the shower as kind of sexy. What were the floors like?"

"Oh, the bathroom was ceramic. The main part had dark hardwood planks. There was a carpet on the floor that didn't quite fit with the furnishings. It looked foreign." A sudden jolt of recognition raced through Jake's body. "Dani, that's it!"

"That's what, Jake? The carpet didn't fit with the rest of the furnishings?"

"No, that's what's been bothering me. Remember I said I saw the man that looked like the accountant yesterday? He must have disappeared into one of the surrounding buildings, but when I looked, I couldn't find him. Some buildings were locked, and some I could only get into the entrance to the lobby. One building had an enclosed display cabinet with business names listed in the entrance. One business sold Turkish rugs. Remember me talking about the rugs that caught my eye at the Bed and Breakfast? A colleague at the paper wrote an article about rugs a while back, and the ones at the B&B could have been Turkish. It has the vibes of a weird coincidence if the man I saw was the guy at the Bed and Breakfast. How many times have you told me you don't believe in coincidences? I need to investigate this. It's a long shot, but maybe there's a connection between the accountant and the rug company."

CHAPTER TWENTY-ONE

JAKE WAS EAGER to get off the phone. He detected skepticism in Dani's voice, although she didn't come out and say anything. He had to admit, the more he talked about linking the rugs to the accountant, the more far-fetched it sounded to him, too. A connection between the accountant and the rug company could be a reach too far. Jake was pretty certain the man he saw was the accountant but not 100 percent sure. Still, hunches paid off for him during his career more often than not.

As soon as he disconnected with a promise to call Dani back after his trip downtown and her reminder to follow up with his pregnant daughter, Jake searched for the article his colleague wrote about rugs made in other countries. A couple of clicks with his mouse and he found it. It revealed that aside from Persian rugs made in Iran, buyers consider Turkish handmade rugs to be the most popular design in the world. The article noted the rugs are well-respected for their durability and unique designs. He searched in his browser for Turkish rugs and noted designs similar to those placed throughout the Bed and Breakfast.

Another idea occurred to Jake. He Googled the surname of the B&B owners. It turned out that Demir is a common Turkish name. Again, he thought he might be onto something. Or it all could be coincidence.

He Googled Turkish rug businesses in Ottawa and found the usual big box stores and a handful of independents. One of the latter was called Ottawa Independent Turkish Rugs with an address on Sparks Street. Jake recognized the name as the one he saw in the building downtown. Their website was sparse but included enough detail to shock Jake at the eye-popping prices.

Jake experienced the familiar surge of excitement. Ready to resume his search downtown, he checked on Oliver again to see the cat sitting on his perch in the kitchen, eyeing a blue jay sneak seed from the feeder in the front yard before the squirrel came and ruined the party. The cat seemed content, so Jake grabbed his jacket, pressed the garage door opener, and headed out to retrieve his car. There would be no need for the jacket as the late morning temperature closed in on 30 degrees Celsius.

The air conditioner pumped cool air into the car's interior. Jake followed the same route he took the day before, even parking at the World Exchange Plaza in a spot next to the one he had parked in. The Plaza housed two office towers and occupied a city block. He rode the elevator to the main floor, hurried through the east entrance and up the stairs toward Sparks Street. It didn't take long to arrive at the building housing the Turkish rug company. He confirmed the name Ottawa Independent Turkish Rugs in raised white lettering on a black background behind the glass display. The sign showed the office number on the second floor.

Jake nodded to the security guard and took the stairs two at a time. His heart pounded, partially from the exertion but more from the excitement of what he might find. The store's name was stenciled on the solidly constructed door that prevented him from seeing inside. He turned the handle on the door, and a chime dinged as he stepped into a large showroom.

The store took up at least half of the second floor. Jake didn't see anyone, so he wandered around the floor space winding between piles of rugs. Enlarged, framed photos of rugs in hallways, dining rooms, and bedrooms adorned the eggshell-colored walls. Jake recognized three from the Bed and Breakfast. The rugs lay piled on top of one another on the floor, and the more expensive ones were hung perpendicular from racks. He checked various price points on the rugs, and they varied widely. None were cheap. Jake decided he wouldn't know a quality rug from a knockoff, but as he noted on the website, most were outrageously expensive. It was an impressive display.

Jake didn't care about the display. He wanted to talk to the man doing the accounting for the business.

"Hello, anyone here?" he shouted.

A voice came from behind one rack, muffled by the rugs. "Just a second, I'll be right out."

Jake separated the rugs where the voice came from to see an open door to a hallway leading farther back into the building. He couldn't see into the office where the voice had apparently come from. He sat on a pile of rugs and waited with his back to the door he expected the owner of the voice to enter through.

Like most people do when they're waiting, he played with his phone. He sent Avery a text message. *Thinking of you, sweetheart. Hope everything is going well.* There was probably some text vocabulary he was supposed to use. Dani's daughter, Emilie, tried to teach him but decided he was a slow learner and gave up. He added a smiley face emoji, along with a heart. He thought that was pretty good for an old timer.

A message came back within seconds. *Hi, Dad. Doing great. Call me when you can.* Doing great. Call me when you can. That was it. What did that mean? Was she really doing great? If so, why did she want him to call her as soon as he could? Was there a problem with her pregnancy? Jake decided he should have asked a question to receive a more complete answer and resolved to call Avery the minute he got home.

He heard the screech of metal on metal behind him as the rings holding the rugs slid along the bar from which they hung. Jake wanted to turn around, but he held his ground as the man's footsteps approached. When he drew near, the man said, "Good morning, sir. Apologies for the delay. I was dealing with a customer on the phone.

Can I help you find a rug that will enhance your living quarters and make you the envy of your friends?"

Jake was certain the man hadn't been talking on the phone, but the hair on his neck stood at attention. He couldn't be sure because the man he saw at the B&B only grunted a few monosyllables, but there were similarities in the cadence. Jake waited until the man stood directly in front of him before he rose from his seat. The man was about Jake's height except for the stooped shoulders. A wave of excitement, satisfaction, and even vindication traveled through Jake as he nodded to the man. The pasty face of the accountant stared back at him.

CHAPTER TWENTY-TWO

THE ACCOUNTANT HAD a ring of hair around the crown of his head, was slight of stature, wore wire-rimmed glasses and sported a mustache. He wore tan dress pants and an open-necked, short-sleeved white shirt with brown pinstripes and reeked of cigarette smoke.

Jake held out his hand. "Good morning, my name is Jake Scott. And you are?"

The accountant recovered enough to pretend he didn't have a clue who Jake was. He shook Jake's hand and replied, "My name is Fletcher Patterson. How can I help you?"

"I think you remember me, Fletcher Patterson. I could tell by your face you recognized me as soon as you saw me. You were at the Sweet Dreams Bed and Breakfast the morning of the explosion. Obviously, you checked out before the blast. The strange thing is that your name wasn't on the guest list."

"Who are you, and why should I talk to you? How did you find me, anyway?"

"Like I said, my name's Jake Scott, and I'm a retired reporter. A friend at the police department asked me to do some preliminary investigation. That's why I'm here. If it turns out the explosion was deliberate, they're going to investigate in much more depth, so it's in your best interests to tell me everything you know so I can pass it on. I played a hunch because of the rugs at the B&B. I saw you yesterday, and when you disappeared, I assumed you entered a nearby building. Low and behold, a business in one building sells Turkish rugs, and here we are. Did you know Omar and Seda Demir? Since you weren't on the guest list, I assume you did."

Patterson hesitated for the briefest of moments, locking eyes with Jake before replying, "I knew them. Let's go back into the office. I'll show you something."

Jake and Patterson wound their way through the rugs and open doorway into a tiny cube of an office about the size of a large bathroom. Stacks of paper lay along the walls and on the desk. A gray laptop sat open on the desk among the clutter, and an ancient gray metal filing cabinet stood left of the chair. Paint peeled on the eggshell-colored walls, and the source of the cigarette smoke became evident as an overflowing ashtray teetered on the edge of the desk. Cigarette butts, smoked to the end, littered the floor by the chair. No Turkish rug protected the cheap plank flooring. The nonexistent air circulation left Jake with an immediate claustrophobic sensation. The walls seemed to close in even more with the clutter in the room.

Patterson removed sheets of paper from the guest chair and gestured for Jake to sit. The accountant tossed the papers on the bulging cabinet and squeezed between the wall and the desk to get to the chair opposite Jake. He shook a cigarette from a pack but thought better of it. Instead, he clicked the top of a pen.

Click. Click.

Patterson said, "I knew the Demirs. I have for years. I liked them. Or at least I did until I found out something that disturbed me."

Jake removed his phone from his pocket. "Do you mind if I record this? My memory isn't as sharp as it used to be." With Patterson's agreement, Jake hit the record button and placed the phone on the desk. He said, "Do you think the blast was an accident, Fletcher?"

"I don't know. I have my suspicions." Patterson's lips moved as if to say something more, but he paused.

"Go on," Jake encouraged.

Click. Click. Click.

"Seda owned this rug store. I've been the accountant for about ten years. They've been having financial difficulty with the store for several years. It's a good thing they owned the Bed and Breakfast to help pay off their debts, but it didn't generate enough money. The lenders were getting agitated."

Jake's mind drifted to the price of the expensive rugs and couldn't help but think it must be a specialized market with few buyers. He tuned back in as Patterson continued.

"I enjoyed working for them. Despite their financial difficulties, they paid me well. Now, I'm wrapping up their estate. Their relatives are all in Turkey. They asked me to do this when I called them. I'll be holding a liquidation sale."

"You seemed to be out of sorts at breakfast. Was something bothering you?" Jake studied Patterson's thumb on the top of the pen as he pressed faster with each question.

"Yeah, I discovered some irregularities with the rugs and confronted Seda with the information that morning before all of you came down for breakfast. She and Omar got angry, but they told me to sit down and eat breakfast, so we could continue the conversation after everyone left. I couldn't stomach breakfast, so I left. I went back in the evening but got nowhere with them despite the evidence I showed them. That's the last time I spoke to either of them. They made me mad for deceiving me all those years. If the police check my phone records, they'll find out the Demirs called my cell phone a couple of times that day, but I never answered. I was too angry. Or maybe embarrassed."

"What irregularities?"

Patterson finally set the annoying pen down and lifted a sheet of paper from the top of the pile. It was an invoice, and he pointed to the company name at the top. "See this name?"

The name meant nothing to Jake. "Yes, but what's the significance?"

Patterson pointed to a unit cost dollar figure for ten rugs purchased for the store. It wasn't in the same universe as the price listed on some rugs in the showroom.

Jake said, "Based on the price of the rugs out front, there must be a huge markup. I understand shipping costs would add to it, but still…"

"That's what I always thought. If the Demirs had done proper advertising, which I always encouraged them to do, they could have made a killing. They were always reluctant to set up a proper website or lease a location with a visible storefront where people driving by would notice. I told myself the rugs were handmade by kids in Turkey who make fifteen bucks a month or something. That would account for the low unit cost. I have always wanted to visit that part of the world, so I traveled to Turkey during my holidays. I went to the address on the invoice and guess what?"

Jake stared to see where this was going. He said, "It doesn't exist."

With a deep sigh, Patterson ran a hand across his bald head to wipe off perspiration that had accumulated. "You're right, it doesn't exist. I took some of the paperwork with me and tracked the origin of the rugs to a factory in Ankara from the shipping labels. I found out the rugs aren't handmade. They're mass-produced. They're worth about a tenth of the price the Demirs have been putting on them for the last ten years. The quality of the rugs is still damn good, but they're not handmade, and that's what Seda sold them as." The color rose in Patterson's cheeks. "When I confronted the Demirs about it, they didn't deny it. It was like they thought the buyers needed to be more careful. They blamed it all on the people buying the rugs. I could lose my accounting license if the governing bodies ever found out I've been involved in fraud for ten years. I'll liquidate the stock for a fraction of the selling price. I felt humiliated, and the Demirs laughed at first and then got angry."

"It sounds like you could have been angry enough to want some kind of revenge. Did you blow up the B&B, Fletcher? Were you humiliated enough to get rid of the Demirs?"

"Of course not. I couldn't do such a thing. There might be people who would, though."

"Oh, yeah? Who?"

"I told you the Demirs mortgaged the store to the hilt. I think there are other stores in Canada selling the same knockoff rugs, and they're all financed by the same people."

"Like?" It was like pulling teeth.

"The Demirs paid exorbitant interest rates for their loans to keep the store afloat. I think owners in other cities did the same. As soon as I liquidate the remaining rugs, I'm leaving town." Patterson leaned across the desk, lowering his voice. "I think it's all part of an organized crime network. These are bad people who might have wanted to send a message to others that owe them money by blowing up the Bed and Breakfast."

CHAPTER TWENTY-THREE

THINGS HAD JUST taken a right-hand turn. If organized crime were involved, the explosion could have been deliberate, and if the purpose was to send a message, they wouldn't care about collateral damage. It would explain the nagging question about why anyone would deliberately cause a blast that would kill several people. Jake shuddered at the thought.

Patterson shifted uncomfortably in his seat. His face grew paler as a bead of sweat originating on his forehead trickled down his cheek. Jake wondered if the man thought he had said too much, but he sensed there was more. Something Patterson was reluctant to say. Jake asked, "Did you see anyone else at the B&B before you left?"

The accountant cleared his throat, about to say something when the chime tinkled, and the door closed in the showroom. Patterson's eyes shifted to the right and down. Jake noticed a small security monitor sitting on a corner of the cluttered desk to the right of the laptop and behind a pile of papers.

"Yes, but someone's here," Patterson said. "Maybe I can sell one of these godforsaken rugs. I'll call you. I've got your number." He stood and withdrew a business card from a brown sports jacket draped over the back of his chair. He squeezed between the wall and the desk and waited for Jake to stand as he handed him the card.

For his part, Jake realized he was being dismissed, took the business card, and preceded Patterson through the door and into the main area where a tall, overweight, middle-aged man wearing brown shorts and a yellow golf shirt waited. Patterson jovially greeted the man as if Jake had already left and asked if he could interest him in a beautiful carpet manufactured in Turkey. Jake noted Patterson omitted "handmade" from his introduction.

Since lunchtime approached, Jake wandered back to the World Exchange Plaza, sat on a bench, and called Dani. When she answered, he said, "I'm downtown on Metcalfe, and I have news. I found the accountant who told me some interesting things. Can you spare a few minutes for a quick sandwich? I can meet you on Elgin Street."

"Sure, but since you're on Metcalfe Street, why don't we meet at the Colonnade Pizza in about ten minutes? I haven't eaten pizza in, oh, two days now."

They agreed on pizza, and Jake set out on foot, heading south toward the restaurant. He hustled down the street, past the Ottawa Public Library, various apartment hotels and businesses, and the Greek Embassy to arrive at the restaurant about two minutes before the agreed-upon time. He claimed a seat on the sidewalk patio facing the direction Dani would come from and waited.

She strode down the street with her head up, and for Jake, it was like the sun just came out. Something about her quickened his pulse. He didn't know what it was, but he liked it.

She wore business attire of cobalt blue dress pants and a matching jacket with a white shirt. Her shoes were darker blue casual wedge loafers, and a black bag hung over her shoulder. Despite her relatively short stature, her long strides put a hitch in her step, which caused her black hair to bounce on her shoulders. When she noticed Jake, she waved and beamed that gorgeous wide smile that pumped up his heart rate. He watched her enter the front door of the building and disappear for a few minutes. When she returned to his line of sight, she spoke to the server and pointed in Jake's direction with a smile. She emerged on the patio, headed for the table Jake had chosen, and leaned down with one hand on his shoulder, kissing him on the cheek. Jake stood to pull her chair back to sit, but she waved him off.

Dani apologized for her side trip to the washroom before coming to the table, and they chatted amiably while consulting on their menus. They selected a medium combination pizza with no anchovies, a Corona for her, and a Coors Light for him. They clinked bottles for no particular reason when the two beers arrived.

While they waited for the pizza, Dani said, "So, it sounds like you had a productive morning. Tell me about the meeting with the accountant."

"What a nervous guy. He looked sick when he figured out who I was, and he smokes like a chimney. He was about to light a cigarette in the office but thought better of it for some reason. The ashtray already overflowed. He gave the top of a pen a real workout while he talked. He had a lot to say, and he didn't finish. Someone came into the store before he revealed everything. He said someone else was at the B&B that night, but that was it. I'll follow up with him."

Jake handed Dani his phone, and she listened to his conversation with Patterson wearing the earbuds he provided. The pizza arrived as she listened, and Jake waited. Her expression changed little until, Jake assumed, the possibility of organized crime involvement came up. That prompted a raised eyebrow.

When she finished, she handed the phone back to Jake and slid a lifter under two pieces of pizza to place them on their plates. Jake took a bite and asked, "What do you think? That could explain the reason for taking out an entire house full of people."

"It could. Something else Patterson said intrigued me. He implied the store bled money. He's an accountant, so he would not want that to happen. It sounded like he tried to convince the Demirs to at least improve their advertising and storefront to bring in more customers, and they didn't agree. Why would they continue operating and almost sabotaging themselves by not taking measures to improve things? It sounds like a terrible business plan."

Jake washed a mouthful of pizza down with a swallow of beer. "Patterson said they paid him well despite their financial problems, so maybe his efforts to improve the operation were half-hearted. He got what he wanted, which was to make money."

Raucous laughter from another table interrupted their conversation. Dani leaned forward. "Yes, Jake, but he would've realized his cushy job would end if something didn't improve. He would've seen the writing on the wall."

"That's true. Maybe they just wouldn't listen, and he rode it out as long as possible. He's a relatively young man. He could get a job somewhere else."

Dani lifted her last piece of pizza onto her plate. "I must have been famished. I normally don't eat that much pizza for lunch. My eyes will be drooping this afternoon. Beer and too much pizza do that. Think it through a little more, Jake. There could be another reason they kept the place going despite losing money."

Jake asked the server for a box to take home his last piece of pizza. He drained the last of his beer as he tried to read Dani's mind. Then, a flash of insight.

"Money laundering."

"Yup. That's what I'm thinking. They paid Patterson well for a job at a sinking company. Why do that? Patterson said the Demirs's store was only one of a few in the country selling the same products. They could all be losing money, fronts for laundering money from criminal activity."

Jake tapped his card on the machine held by the server to pay for their meals. He asked, "What do you want me to do next? So far, we have the owners of the Bed and Breakfast, who may have been involved in money laundering and up to their ears in debt to an alleged organized crime outfit, and a pregnant woman scared enough by a Member of Parliament that she needed to hide. The accountant, Patterson, also told me he had more to say. Probably about the other person at the

B&B. We still have no proof the explosion was deliberate, so all of this could end up being nothing."

Dani got up from her chair. "I must run, Jake. I don't want you getting too deeply into this, especially if organized crime is involved. Please send me your recorded discussion with Patterson, and I'll forward the file to the Fraud Unit. They're dedicated to solving crimes like this. Investigate around the edges. Call the accountant if you want to find out what he wants to tell you and let me know. Don't go any further with that. If you want to do more, look into the military guy and his wife to find out what their story is. You can decide whether you continue."

Jake hugged Dani and walked her to the street corner. As she turned to walk back to work, Jake said, "Are you kidding? What else would I do? Oliver and I can only tolerate each other for so long. This gives me an excuse to get out of the house."

CHAPTER TWENTY-FOUR

JAKE DAWDLED ON his way back to his car. The buildings on either side of the street, the cars drifting by, the construction equipment pounding the sidewalk with a pneumatic hammer opposite the side he walked on, and the people he met or who hurried past him, didn't register. Deep thoughts occupied his mind.

Dani's suggestion of money laundering intrigued him. From what he knew, the practice would involve passing money through the rug store to some other enterprise. The store would deposit much more cash than the sales figures would support and invest the excess in some legitimate business, such as real estate. They wouldn't care if they sold rugs. Jake heard it referred to as "layering." Multiple transactions would be involved in a complicated process to avoid tax implications and hide money from the authorities. It would require an accountant who understood what he was doing. An accountant like Fletcher Patterson.

If Dani was right, Patterson had *much* more to tell Jake than he had so far. That could explain the reason for his nervousness. If he were about to come clean, he could put his life in danger; if the crime syndicate knew, they might have hoped to eliminate the Demirs and Patterson at the same time. Anybody else lost in the blast would be collateral damage. It was another workable theory. When the Syndicate found out Patterson survived, he could be the next target.

Jake considered the money laundering angle all the way home, leaning more and more to organized crime being responsible if the blast turned out to be deliberate. But Dani was right. He hadn't investigated the military man, Craig Thorpe, and his wife, Francis. He planned to make phone calls when he got home. He would follow up if Patterson didn't call by tomorrow evening. As the garage door rolled up, and he drove the car into the space, he remembered that first, he had to check on Avery.

Oliver greeted him at the door with mild curiosity. The cat rolled onto his back, the universal sign of feline trust and confidence. Jake rubbed Oliver's tummy until the cat became impatient and hurried to his bowl, nudging it around the floor with his paw. Jake took the hint, retrieved Oliver's food out of the closet, and filled the bowl, shoving the cat aside to do so. As soon as he finished, Oliver dove in as if he hadn't eaten for a week.

Jake left the cat in the kitchen and wandered into the sunroom, dialing his phone as he walked. Avery picked up on the second ring. "How's it going, honey?" he asked.

"Good, Dad. I've been nauseous a few mornings but nothing serious. I've been reading online about the side effects of pregnancy in my free time."

Jake sat in his lounge chair. "Nausea? Is everything okay?" He realized his voice ticked up an octave.

"Geez, Dad. Where were you when I was born? It's perfectly normal. Nothing to worry about."

"Well, okay. That's what Dani said, too. I've forgotten what it was like when your mom was pregnant with you. That was a long time..." His voice trailed off as he realized Avery might not appreciate his pointing out she was getting older. He changed the subject. "Are you sure researching the internet is something you want to do, though? The health-care professionals seem to want us to avoid self-diagnosis. Something about a little knowledge being a dangerous thing." Jake chuckled.

"Yeah, well, that's what they say, but the health-care system sucks right now, as you know, so we get our information when and where we can. I'm lucky to have an excellent obstetrician, and she says everything is going along normally. Anyway, enough about me. What's new with you? How's your case going?"

Jake pushed the lever on his chair to tilt back. He sensed he was about to become on a "need to know" basis regarding the pregnancy. A brief jolt of jealousy shot through him as he thought of Nick hearing everything from Avery as and when it happened. He experienced the same reaction as they drove away when they moved to Toronto. He didn't like it, but life evolves. *Why do the years go by so fast?*

"Ha ha! It's not really my 'case,' as you know, dear. I'm helping Dani with some preliminary investigations. We still don't know if the blast was accidental, but there are a couple of people who could have been targets if it was deliberate." He told her about meeting Willow Altman and her involvement with the Member of Parliament, Dan Rivera. The Fletcher Patterson sighting downtown and deducing that he worked for the rug company came up. His pride at his deduction was probably obvious. He left out Willow's pregnancy and Patterson's suggestion about organized crime or that money laundering might be involved. He didn't want to panic his daughter into thinking he was getting in over his head yet again.

"Okay, Dad, I must run. It's been great talking to you. Promise me you won't get too involved with this case or whatever it is. I know you. It's like your nose is to the ground, and you're sniffing something rotten. I can hear it in your voice. Leave the proper investigations to the experts."

"I promise I won't get too involved." Jake thought that should leave him enough wiggle room to explain his way out of trouble with his daughter if anything too serious happened.

They hung up, and Jake stayed tilted back on his chair. From his vantage point, he watched the birds at the backyard feeder, which needed replenishing. Two brilliant yellow American goldfinches flitted about the feeder. Oliver sauntered into the room and plunked himself down on the carpet in front of Jake's chair. He never showed much interest in the backyard feeder. It always perplexed Jake as he watched the slumbering cat now. Maybe the cat thought the daily battle between the blue jay and the squirrel in the front yard was much more entertaining than the smaller birds at the backyard feeder. Or maybe the plumpness of the blue jay and squirrel attracted Oliver as he dreamed about having one or both for lunch.

Jake considered Avery's admonishment to leave the case alone. Maybe she was right. The last two cases he helped Dani with almost cost him his life. This one felt different, though. As Dani said, he was only chipping away at the edges, so the chances of getting into a life-threatening situation were between slim and none. Besides, he felt alive when he contributed to something. He supposed if he wasn't doing this, he would volunteer for a service organization to stay busy, but he could do that later. This was more exciting.

He admitted to himself that speaking with Avery left him melancholy. Another reminder that time marches on, not stopping for anyone. If anything, time picked up momentum every day as he trooped through life. Suddenly, a temperamental, slightly overweight, furry animal joined him. Oliver, who rarely showed affection, except maybe to Dani's daughter, Emilie, had leaped onto his lap and curled into a comfortable position.

Jake stroked the cat's fur and said, "What do you think, Oliver? Should I stop this nonsense and volunteer somewhere?"

The cat responded with a loud purr and drooping eyes.

"I didn't think so, either. Let's take a few minutes and then see what we can find on Craig and Francis Thorpe."

With that, they both fell asleep.

CHAPTER TWENTY-FIVE

JAKE WOKE BEFORE Oliver and nudged the disgruntled cat off his lap. He felt refreshed and wandered into his office. He glanced at his whiteboard as he sat in his chair and reminded himself about the Thorpes's lack of acquaintances on social media. Three each, in fact. He drilled down into the friends' social media pages to discover that two of Craig's friends worked in the military, and two of Francis's were military wives. The personal page of one showed she was a friend to both Craig and Francis and provided a link to a bookstore in Petawawa, Ontario, the town where the military base was located.

A click on the link took Jake to a page describing the bookstore, how its owners serve the 6,100 members of Garrison Petawawa, an order page urging customers to purchase any of its 22,000 books, and a contact page, including a phone number. Jake picked up his phone and dialed.

A female answered, identifying the store, and asking how she could help.

"Hi," Jake said. "I would like to speak to Kristy Bedard, please."

"I'm sorry. Kristy is home sick today. Can I help you?"

"No, thank you. It's a personal matter. It's urgent that I speak with her, though. Is there some way you could put me in touch with her?"

The girl obviously debated how to handle his question, judging by the brief silence that followed. Then, "If you tell me what this is about, I'll call Kristy and ask her to contact you."

"Okay, that works for me. I noticed on social media that Kristy was a friend of Craig and Francis Thorpe, who unfortunately died in the explosion at the Bed and Breakfast in Ottawa. I'm doing a preliminary investigation on behalf of the Ottawa Police Service, and I'm looking for background information about the Thorpes. If Ms. Bedard could call me back as soon as possible, I would appreciate it."

The woman said, "That was so horrible about those people. I didn't know them, but the news shook Kristy up. I'll call her right away and ask her to call you back."

"That would be very helpful. Thank you so much." Jake gave the young woman his name and phone number and hung up.

He leaned back in his chair, his legs stretched in front of him, and his hands behind his head. The young lady would be more likely to pass along his message since he left out the part about being a former reporter. He wasn't sure reporters, or anything related to them, would be welcome around anyone connected with the military.

His phone rang a few minutes later. Jake unwound his hands from behind his head, leaned forward to tap the key to answer and another to put it on speaker. It was Kristy Bedard.

The woman sounded like she was on her deathbed. Her voice cracked with a nasal undertone, and she cleared her throat when she spoke. She croaked, "How can I help you?"

Jake reiterated the information he gave the young lady at the bookstore and added, "I saw your name on the social media pages for both Craig and Francis Thorpe. I want to offer my sincere condolences for your loss. I was staying at the B&B at the same time and met them at breakfast. Luckily, I wasn't there when the explosion occurred, but I feel terrible for the people killed in the blast.

"Craig and Francis seemed to be nice people. I'm doing a

preliminary investigation on behalf of the Ottawa Police Service, so I'm talking to people who may have known the victims. I hope you can tell me a little about them."

Kristy blew her nose away from the phone before saying, "I'm sorry. There's nothing worse than a cold in the summer. Why is there an investigation? Wasn't it an accidental gas explosion?"

"That's the working theory, Kristy. A friend at the Ottawa Police Service asked me to investigate things preliminarily so no stone is left unturned, if I may use that expression. What can you tell me about the Thorpes?"

"I was so sad to hear the news. Craig and I went to school together in British Columbia. He was a good man, and I liked him. We were like brother and sister. He'd been deployed a few times. He married Francis before he moved here, but he changed. Much quieter and more reserved. Deployments can do that to a person, but it always seemed to me the reason was Francis. Call it women's intuition.

"Francis often came into the bookstore when Craig was deployed, but she wasn't a warm person. We never connected. It was almost like she was jealous of me because I was friends with Craig. I'm not sure why she friended me on social media unless she wanted to keep track of me in case I had something going on with her husband. I didn't, of course. She had few actual friends I know of. I never saw her with anyone, and she never participated in any town activities. They have their own things on the base, so maybe she was more involved there. I would see Craig having coffee in town or shopping when he was home. We would have coffee together sometimes. He was still friendly and outgoing but more reserved. His wife never seemed happy at all."

Kristy waited for a beat before saying with a sigh, "I might as well tell you I'm not being completely honest. Craig suffered from Post-Traumatic Stress Disorder. His personality had changed a lot when I saw him last. His marriage was falling apart. He seemed to have no use for Francis anymore. That pleased me because I thought Francis was a witch. Still, the new Craig scared me a little sometimes. His eyes were vacant; he'd lose concentration. A sudden noise would startle him, and he would become furious. That all happened a couple of times over a coffee. He was on leave and undergoing counseling."

Jake's mind harkened back to the breakfast. He recalled that Craig had done all the talking, but he was fidgety. He couldn't sit still. The only words Francis spoke were when she greeted him. Jake just attributed it to shyness.

The thought flashed through Jake's head that the opposite of what Kristy said could be true. Maybe Kristy was jealous of Francis. He probed further.

"I don't want to keep you on the phone, Kristy. You should be resting, but I have a couple more questions. Could you please elaborate on your impressions of Francis?"

Kristy cleared her throat for what seemed like the tenth time before answering. "I tried to start a conversation once. As I'm sure you know, military people move around a lot, so one time, when she came into the store, I asked where their last deployment was. She said, 'British Columbia.' Obviously, I know B.C., so I said, 'Oh, the base at Comox?' She asked why I was being so nosy! Can you imagine? I just tried to be friendly, and it was like I asked for her bank account information."

"Hmm… I suppose she could have reacted like that for a reason. Could security be an explanation? The need to keep it secret?"

"Yes, of course, that's a possibility. I assumed she was being rude, so I let it go with the intention of never talking to her again any more than necessary. But when the explosion happened, I called Craig's mom to offer my condolences. She still lives in B.C. His dad passed a few years ago. She was inconsolable, of course. We talked for quite a while, but she didn't mention Francis for most of the conversation, which I thought kind of odd.

"We talked for a while longer, and when we were about to hang up, she said something that shocked me." Jake waited as a rustling sound came over the phone. Kristy found another tissue as Jake heard her blowing her nose again. He felt awful for keeping her on the phone this long. It sounded like she was on the verge of pneumonia.

When Kristy returned, she said, "I'm so sorry about this. Where was I?"

"You said Craig's mother said something shocking."

"Oh, yes. Sorry. Craig's mom is the kindest, gentlest person I've ever met. I spent time at their place growing up, and she was the most wonderful person. When my mom passed, Craig's mom took over. She never said a bad word about anyone. That's why what she said shocked me so much. I remember her words as if she said them two minutes ago. She said, 'It should have just been Francis in the explosion. If anyone in that building deserved to die, it was Francis.'"

CHAPTER TWENTY-SIX

JAKE ASKED FOR Craig Thorpe's mother's phone number, which Kristy provided. "Anything I can do to help," she croaked before she hung up with another apology for her cold.

Now Jake stood staring at the rubble that had once been the Bed and Breakfast. He intended to call Thorpe's mom, but the three-hour time zone difference between Ontario and British Columbia left him time to do that before it became too late for the woman. He suddenly needed to get out of the house for a few minutes. He started out in the opposite direction, but something turned him around and propelled him to see what remained after the blast.

A yellow tractor with a front-end loader huffed as it shifted debris from the pile of rubble onto a gravel truck. The truck rocked and sagged further on its springs with each load from the tractor's bucket at the end of its extended articulated arms. A second truck rumbled behind the first, waiting to pull in as soon as the first truck was filled. Hammers echoed up and down the street, as construction workers repaired damaged houses. Soon, it would be as if nothing ever happened except for the loss felt by the loved ones of the victims. Nothing but a vacant lot would be left for the owners' estate to decide what happened next.

Jake marveled at everything that had transpired in a short period. The work at the house that compelled him to move to a Bed and Breakfast that happened to blow up. The lives lost and the things his investigation uncovered. He shook his head at the collection of people who had stayed at the B&B. All seemingly innocent, yet all with secrets in their past. Who knows what he would uncover when he called Craig Thorpe's mom? Maybe nothing, but there must be some reason she thought the way she did of Francis Thorpe and wished it was only her who died.

As the tractor puffed grayish smoke into the air and the truck sagged with each bucket load, he wondered again at the providence that spared him from joining the others in the morgue. Had he not stayed for a drink with his fellow pickleball players, he would have been asleep in the house at the time of the explosion. It was dumb luck, he concluded, but more than ever, he needed to find out what happened. It was a heavy burden as he turned with slumped shoulders to return home to make the next phone call.

His phone vibrated in his pocket, interrupting his thoughts about halfway home. His spirits lifted a bit when he heard Dani's voice. As usual, she picked up on his mood when he answered.

"What are you up to?" she said. "I heard a car go by. Are you outside? Is something wrong?"

"Yeah, I went for a walk. I spoke to a friend of the Thorpes, and it got me down. I had to get some fresh air. I ended up at the site of the blast. They're already clearing up the area. How are you doing?"

Dani ignored the question. "What about your phone call to Thorpe's friend got you down?"

Jake related Kristy's comment about Thorpe's mom. He added, "Everyone staying at the B&B had skeletons in their closet. More and more, a few people might have had reason to set the blast deliberately. Craig Thorpe's PTSD to add to the mix. But why would someone do that when there were a bunch of people inside? What's wrong with people?" He realized as he said it that Dani, more than anyone, saw the worst of humanity as a homicide detective but still wouldn't be able to answer.

"Maybe you should stand down, Jake. It sounds like this is getting to you."

"I can't do that, Dani. I owe the victims something for being the only survivor. Well, me and the accountant. Patterson. I'm going to call Thorpe's mom to see what she has to say."

"Okay, I understand, Jake. I'm not sure the reason for my call will make you feel any better. Since you saw that the debris from the blast is being removed, you probably realized the Fire Marshall concluded his investigation, at least the onsite visit. It wasn't conclusive.

"To give you an idea of what they did, according to the report, they thoroughly walked the scene. They followed the gas system from the street to the house and checked connections on all appliances. Apparently, there's more left after an explosion, even like that one, than you would expect. I've seen them measuring, sketching, and taking pictures at other sites. They're extremely thorough.

"There was a new electric washer and dryer in the basement, but the connection for a gas hookup remained. We'll follow up, of course, but my guess is the owners replaced the natural gas washer and dryer with electric. Maybe they were climate conscious. The problem is the valve leading to the gas hookup hadn't been capped and was in the open position, so natural gas flowed when there was no call for it. Something ignited the gas. A spark, candle… something. I'll have one of my detectives investigate the appliance purchase to see when it happened, but the report implies it wasn't the day of the explosion."

"You say the report is inconclusive. Do you mean because the valve was open? Someone must've opened it deliberately. Why isn't that conclusive?"

"Yes, it was open, but who opened it? Was it left that way by the installer that day? Could've been accidental. Patterson told you someone else was at the B&B. The installer back to do more work? Until we find out when they installed the appliances, we won't know for sure. You didn't see any installers, so it was likely before you moved in, which would've made it more than a few days ago. There's one thing, though. It turns out one of the neighbor's doorbell cameras picked up something interesting before the explosion. The house was farther down the street, and it's a blurred image, but when the team enhanced it, the man walking down the street from the Bed and Breakfast appears to be hunched over as if he had a sore back."

Jake and Dani said the words at the same time.

"The accountant."

CHAPTER TWENTY-SEVEN

DANI SAID IF the appliances had been installed a few days before the blast, there was enough evidence to suggest the explosion may have been intentional, and a formal investigation would be opened. She said, "The open valve cinched it. It wouldn't open itself and wouldn't have sat in the open position for days without someone smelling the rotten egg odor or the house blowing up. Someone must've opened it shortly before the blast. The Fire Marshall's Office will continue to investigate the cause of the explosion, but I want to assign one of my investigators as well. I want to get ahead of this. We'll work with the Fire Marshall's Office like other cases. Between us, we'll determine when the gas appliances were removed and if someone sent a maintenance man out the day of the blast who may have opened the valve or failed to cap the line by accident. You've been very helpful with your investigation so far, Jake, and I really appreciate it. We may need to cover the same ground to make it official, but you've narrowed things down for us. I know you want to continue doing what you're doing, and I won't stop you, but if you feel the need to step back, I'll understand."

Jake took a few seconds to consider Dani's comment, but he had already made up his mind. "I'm going to talk to Thorpe's mom, and I expect Patterson will call. He said he would. Then, I'll leave you to it, Dani."

"Okay, dear, I'll talk to you later, okay? Oh wait, there's one more thing. The Chief is holding a press conference about the explosion this afternoon. You'll be able to catch the highlights on the evening news. There'll be more in the papers tomorrow."

"Do you know what he's going to say?"

Dani chuckled. "You know how these things work. Media Relations wrote what he's going to say. He'll talk about the Fire Marshall's investigation. He won't go into a lot of detail. It's more to suggest there's no danger to the public and that the investigation is ongoing."

"So, it's the 'say a lot while saying nothing' challenge. I'm sure the public is eager to listen to what he has to say."

They concluded their phone call, and Jake shuffled papers on his desk until he found the yellow sticky pad on which he had written Thorpe's mother's name. Halfway through dialing, his phone vibrated in his hand. The display reflected "unknown number," but Jake expected a call from Patterson, so he answered. It was Willow Altman's friend Julie Tremblay instead.

"I'm sorry to bother you, Mr. Scott, but I'm just wondering if you spoke with Rivera, the so-called upstanding Member of Parliament."

"Please call me Jake, Julie. Yes, I spoke with him. He said the baby isn't his, but he admitted to the affair, which he said he was breaking off. I don't know if he had anything to do with Willow's death, but there's no question he is not a very nice guy."

"Willow's baby isn't his? That's surprising and I'm not sure believable. He's despicable, Jake. I did more digging. The rumor mill is rampant around here and accurate more than half the time. There was an office administrator rumored to have had an affair with Rivera, so I took her for coffee. She didn't want to say anything at first, but when I told her about your investigation and said maybe it would avenge Willow's death, she opened up. She confirmed a fling with Rivera, and he was violent toward her. She was about to break it off, but he did first. He told her he would kill her if she said anything to anyone. Those were her exact words, Jake. I asked her to repeat it. He said he would *kill* her."

The temperature in Jake's office seemed to drop ten degrees. "How long ago was this?" he asked.

"She was the last of his conquests before Willow. Who knows how many before that? The guy is a player who should be put down like a rabid animal."

"Okay, Julie. Can you give me her name? I'll either follow up with her or pass the name along to the police."

"She doesn't want to talk to the police, Jake. The whole situation scares her. She said she would talk to you but is afraid of Rivera, especially now. She believes Rivera wouldn't stop at anything to protect his name and reputation. She'll talk to you, but she'll insist that it goes no further."

Julie obviously loathed the man, so the lengths to which she seemed willing to go to bring him down concerned Jake. Maybe too far. But he had to at least follow up with the new lead. He said, "I can't promise anything, Julie. Obviously, I'm obliged to pass her name along to the police if it comes to that."

"She asked that I give her your contact information, but I wanted to check with you first. She promised to contact you. I'll give her your name and number if it's okay with you."

"It's fine, Julie. Give her my contact information. Do you think your rumor mill might shed some light on the identity of Willow's baby's father?"

"I wouldn't know where to start on that one, Jake. Sorry. It could be someone outside government. You surprised me when you told me Rivera said it wasn't his."

Disappointment settled on Jake, but Julie was right that the father could be almost anybody. He thanked her and disconnected. He rose from his chair and picked up the dry erase marker. On the whiteboard, he added under Dan Rivera's name, "Witness to Rivera's temper—name unknown—might call."

He dialed Thorpe's mom again, but the phone vibrating in his hand interrupted him for a second time. This time, Patterson's voice came over the line.

"Mr. Scott? Fletcher Patterson. We need to talk."

"I agree we do, Fletcher. Someone saw you hurrying away from the Bed and Breakfast right before it exploded. I would love to hear your explanation for…"

Patterson interrupted. "Not over the phone! Come to the office tonight at 9:00. Call me when you arrive at the building. I'll come down and get you. I'll tell you what you want to know." He hung up.

"Well, okay then," Jake said to the empty room. "I guess I'll meet you at 9:00. Thanks for giving me options."

Oliver, who snoozed at Jake's feet, woke to see whom he was talking to. Seeing no one else in the room, he drifted off to sleep again.

Jake shrugged and glanced at the phone number he had been about to dial. He completed the action this time, and a woman answered at the other end. She sounded too young to be Thorpe's mom. She turned out to be his sister.

"Mom's lying down right now. Can I help?"

"Yes, maybe you can." Jake introduced himself and explained that he was a former reporter who was helping the police. "I want to offer my sincerest condolences on the loss of your brother. It must have been a terrible shock."

"It was, but I don't understand. The police hired a former reporter to investigate? Can't they afford their own investigators? I suppose you're a reporter looking for dirt. I'm not giving you the satisfaction. This has been hard enough on my family without reporters nosing around. You're not the first, but you're the last!"

The woman's agitated voice rose, and the next sound Jake expected was the phone clicking off in his ear. But he heard something else. Another woman's voice in the background. He pressed the phone tighter to his ear to make out the woman's words.

"Is that Mr. Scott? Kristy called earlier to tell me to expect his call. Let me talk to him, dear."

The daughter's voice sounded muffled, Jake assumed, by her hand on the phone. He understood the gist of it. "Are you sure, Mom? I imagine he's looking for dirt about Craig."

"Kristy told me to trust him, dear. Let me speak to him."

A scrabbling noise followed as the phone apparently transferred from the daughter's hand to her mother's. The older woman's voice came on the line.

"Mr. Scott, Craig's friend Kristy told me you might call, and she urged me to cooperate. How can I help?"

Jake reiterated his condolences for her loss and explained who he was and what he wanted. He added, "It sounds odd that the police would ask a civilian to get involved, but I worked as an investigative reporter for the newspaper and had a close working relationship with the police department. A friend of mine is in charge of Homicide at the department, and since they're busy with another case and short-staffed, she asked me to do some preliminary investigation. I'm talking to a few people who might provide background on those who died at the Bed and Breakfast. Kristy told me you didn't get along with your daughter-in-law, and I hoped you could elaborate. Maybe tell me a little about Craig and Francis."

"Craig was in the military, as I'm sure you already know. They deployed him on several postings in dangerous parts of the world. Some of them he couldn't tell me about. He would call to tell me he received orders and would be gone. He called it Special Operations. It wasn't easy for him. Suddenly, he would show up again, finished with his assignment."

Jake scribbled notes on his notepad as Thorpe's mother talked. "Do you know what assignments he would go on, Mrs. Thorpe. Would they put him in any danger back home?"

She paused. "As I said, he called them Special Operations. You know how close-lipped the military is. I had no clue what he did. I was nervous the whole time he was gone. He couldn't contact me when he was away."

"I'll look into it, but could you tell me the work Special Operations does?"

"Oh, dear! It can be anything from hostage rescue and combatting weapons of mass destruction to supporting operations in areas where there is no combat. They can provide defense of diplomacy anywhere in the world at a moment's notice. It's dangerous work, Mr. Scott."

Jake tried it a different way. "Did Craig ever mention enemies he might have made because of the work he did?"

Mrs. Thorpe laughed. "I'm sure he made lots of enemies, but I don't think any would follow him over here, do you?"

"I don't know, Mrs. Thorpe. I'm just trying to touch all the bases. I was told that Craig had PTSD. Is that true?"

"Oh, dear! I hoped that wouldn't come out. Yes, he was on leave from the military. His missions affected him. But one good thing came out of it. He decided to divorce Francis. To me, the person you should investigate is that woman. Craig should never have married her. She's a fake. Only looking out for herself. It wouldn't surprise me if someone tried to kill her, but they killed so many people doing it." She sniffled. "If Craig hadn't married that woman, I think he'd still be alive today."

CHAPTER TWENTY-EIGHT

MRS. THORPE HAD Jake's attention. She was making strong accusations, including calling Francis a fake and suggesting she might have been responsible for the explosion, at least indirectly.

"Go on, Mrs. Thorpe," he said.

"First, her name isn't Francis. It's Brenda. Brenda Rutledge. Does the name sound familiar, Mr. Scott?"

It did, but Jake couldn't place it. It would nag at him if Mrs. Thorpe didn't tell him. She put him out of his misery. "Brenda Rutledge was a nurse in Toronto, or at least she said she was. She'd had some nurse training but not nearly what she claimed to have. Her credentials said she qualified as a nurse partitioner, which would allow her to diagnose and treat illnesses, order and interpret tests, and prescribe medications.

"She wasn't qualified to do any of that. But she got fake credentials somehow and bamboozled the people who hired her. She was no more qualified to do the work she claimed she could than I am, but someone faked her credentials well enough to get her the job. She prescribed medication for patients. One died because of her carelessness. Doctors couldn't believe she had prescribed what she had and investigated. It didn't take them long to discover she was a fake. Of course, the family sued the hospital, but nothing would bring their loved one back. Brenda, or Francis, got away with two years in prison and some psychiatric sessions. She moved out of town and met Craig somewhere. He's a sucker for a sob story. Always has been. He felt sorry for her and took her in like a rescue puppy from an animal shelter."

The more Mrs. Thorpe talked, the more Jake remembered the case. He recalled the uproar when people found out that someone unqualified was allowed to do what she did. And she did it for a while… long enough to kill someone. The courts ruled it manslaughter by negligence.

He said, "You seem convinced that someone would want to harm Francis, er, Brenda. Why, Mrs. Thorpe? You said the family sued the hospital. Did they receive a settlement? Were they not happy with the punishment Brenda received?"

"The family received a settlement, but would you consider that enough, Mr. Scott? Is that enough for what she did? Craig told me before he started talking about divorce that people found out and they might be forced to move from Petawawa. To start fresh again somewhere else. Change their names again. They received death threats from someone who said they knew everything, and that Brenda would pay for her sins. Craig assumed a family member of the man she killed sent them. Craig's friend, Kristy, kept me informed of Francis's comings and goings. The only time she ever saw the woman was at the bookstore. Francis would pick up a book and leave right away for the base. Kristy agreed she was a horrible woman."

"Would you have any of those death threats in your possession, Mrs. Thorpe?"

"I haven't been able to bring myself to go to Craig's house. My daughter has been there. She said the place was in shambles, so she didn't look through everything. There's stuff everywhere. I'm going to go at some point. I can look for them, then."

"Were they email or handwritten notes?"

"Craig said they resembled those letters kidnappers send on TV. Letters cut from a newspaper to form words. Like some kid would do.

He said they came in the mail every second day for two weeks, so there must have been six or seven."

"The police department is going to want to see them and the envelopes if Craig kept them. Do you know when Craig and his wife received the last threatening message?"

"Why, yes, I do. Craig told me about it the day before the explosion. It was shocking, but, in a way, nothing surprised me. I remember what he said word for word. Craig told me the message said, 'This is your last warning. Brenda Rutledge will die soon.'"

CHAPTER TWENTY-NINE

THEY SPOKE FOR a few more minutes. The more she talked, however, the more Craig's mom became distraught. They hung up, leaving Jake alone with his thoughts. He rose from his chair to go to the whiteboard and did a quick two-step to avoid tripping over Oliver. No matter the relationship between Jake and the cat, Oliver always liked to be underfoot. Jake's agile dance step combined with Oliver's quick reflexes ensured the cat remained unscathed, and Jake didn't flatten his nose against the opposite wall.

Jake picked up the dry erase marker and found a remaining blank space on the whiteboard. Scribbles covered the board. He wrote and underlined, Motive. Under that, he wrote in tiny lettering, Fake Rugs (Organized Crime), Revenge (Brenda Rutledge), and Pregnant Girlfriend (Dan Rivera). The list seemed in order of most to least likely motive. Then he added Baby Daddy (Unknown) for the father of Willow's baby. His last entry was Fletcher Patterson's name and the unknown man Patterson talked about as the people who may have caused the explosion. He wondered what Patterson would tell him later in the evening.

Jake stepped back to examine his handwork. It resembled something a three-year-old might do if allowed to unleash his creative talent on the board. If English-speaking aliens landed, they would shake their heads in confusion at the mess on the board and confiscate it for further study.

He glanced at his watch. It read 5:30 p.m. so the evening news would soon be on. He wandered to the kitchen to prepare a meal when a chirp from his phone announced a text message. Dani's seventeen-year-old daughter.

S'up J?

Jake smiled. Emilie's texts always entertained him and were often nearly impossible to decipher. Kind of reminded him of his whiteboard. Whether or not he understood the messages, at least she texted him, which warned his heart. He stored a texting dictionary in "favorites" on his phone to consult as and when needed.

Not much, Em. About to eat something. What are you up to?

Bored asf. Think I need a bf.

Jake shook his head. He knew the "f" stood for the profanity gaining more and more traction in modern communication, and "as" meant what it said. He translated "bf" to boyfriend or best friend. Since she had many best friends, he assumed she was talking about the former.

I think a bf will come, Em. The lasting ones just happen.

Ya think so, J?

I do, Em. Your mom and I just happened. We didn't go looking for each other.

The conversation continued with Emilie's weird texting language and Jake's full sentences. Every one of their texting sessions proceeded that way, and neither of them minded. Emilie informed Jake in her cryptic style that she felt better after chatting with him. Just before six p.m., they ended the conversation with *cya*, which they both understood to mean "see you."

He made a toasted tomato sandwich and heated potato chips in the air fryer during the text exchange. He put the fast food on a plate, which he carried to the sunroom. The news started as he clicked on the TV, sat in his chair, and bit into his sandwich.

The broadcast led with the Chief's press conference. It was still underway as the station switched to a reporter at the scene. The Chief's eyes danced as he read from a script from a teleprompter the way Dani described. Not much information, but reassurance that everything was well in hand and no danger to the public existed. Jake stabbed potato chips with his fork and alternated bites of his sandwich with the tasty fries. His rising cholesterol occurred to him, but he offset that by telling himself since he prepared the chips in the air fryer, it would be okay.

He ate the last chip and wiped his mouth with a napkin as the Chief wrapped up the press conference. Jake picked up his plate to carry it to the kitchen when the Chief's last few sentences caught his attention.

"If anyone has information about the explosion, please call the phone number on the screen. You can remain anonymous, but please inform us if you heard or saw anything. Just today, a person offered information that may help our investigation. We will follow any lead, so please come forward if you know anything at all."

The Chief turned as reporters shouted questions at his back. "Who came forward? What kind of information? Does that mean the explosion was deliberate?"

Jake had the same questions and more. *Who was the Chief talking about? Why didn't Dani mention it when he spoke with her? Maybe they were closer to solving the mystery than he thought.*

He pondered the questions as the newscaster switched to a different item. Jake's phone rang as he wandered to the kitchen with his plate. It was Dani.

"Hi, Jake, did you see the press conference?"

"I just finished watching it, Dani. It ended with a surprise."

"Yes, that wasn't in the script. He adlibbed that part. I think he tried to emphasize the importance of people coming forward and kind of let the cat out of the bag. All he did was raise questions in people's minds. Someone came forward, but I'm not sure how much it will amount to. I don't know how reliable the person is."

Jake held the phone between his shoulder and ear as he opened the door to the dishwasher and leaned forward to place his plate, knife, and fork in the slots. He waited for Dani to continue.

"I know you're dying to know who came forward, Jake. Someone you're sort of familiar with. Remember the legally blind lady that almost ran you down?"

CHAPTER THIRTY

JAKE STOOD UP, incredulous. "You've got to be kidding me. *That's the witness?* Isn't she senile?"

"That's what her son and his wife claim, but she's been calling the station nonstop since about two hours before the press conference saying that she had information. One of my constables talked to her and said she sounded lucid. We might have jumped to conclusions. She's legally blind and took her son's car for a joyride, but that doesn't mean she's senile. I guess we're all guilty of writing the elderly off sooner than we need to sometimes. I talked to her myself. She had some interesting things to say."

"Like what?" Jake asked.

"She claims she saw a man leaving the Bed and Breakfast when she drove by."

Jake snorted. "She didn't see me when I walked across the street. How could she see someone leaving the B&B? I thought she was legally blind."

"She is. I looked up the definition of legally blind, and it means a person can't read standard-sized text at a normal distance. We'll test her eyesight to determine whether she could describe someone from a distance in the dark. I haven't driven down the street you crossed on, but how's the lighting?"

Jake reflected on the night for a moment. "It was late at night, as you know, and I remember seeing my shadow as I walked down the sidewalk. I crossed between streetlights, so it was kind of dark. It was 11:00 at night."

"And what did you wear? Your usual drab middle-aged attire?" Dani chuckled.

"What do you mean *drab*?" He thought again about the night the woman nearly ran him down. "Okay, yeah, my shorts were navy, and my shirt that night was dark gray."

"I rest my case. The lady described the man in a bit of detail. She said he walked beneath a streetlight when she saw him. We have to give her the benefit of the doubt for now. The way she described the man, he wasn't the accountant, for sure. She said she thought he was tall and had long hair. She also said he wore a jacket with white on the sleeve. Maybe paint, she thought. She apologized for her failing eyesight and was sorry she couldn't provide more detail, but she thought she should say something."

Shock traveled the length of Jake's body. "Seriously!? Dani, that sounds like the guy at the hotel I stayed at. Remember, I thought someone watched me? I saw him when I went into the hotel, and then I thought I saw him in a car in the parking lot when you came over. Again, in the restaurant. That guy had a white electrician's logo on his sleeve. He might know enough about natural gas to set off an explosion."

"There's another thing," Dani said. "The old lady's name is Gladis Knight."

"Seriously!?" Jake said again, only this time a little louder. "As in Gladys Knight and the Pips? Gladys from the Motown days?"

"Yes, well, not *that* Gladys. This one spells her name with an 'i' instead of a 'y', and I'm not sure she can carry a tune, but that's her name."

Sarcasm dripped from Jake's voice when he said, "Just keeps getting weirder and weirder. All we need to do now is figure out who that guy was, if he really came from the B&B, and what his motives were. Or if Gladis Knight actually saw someone in the dark."

Dani chuckled. "We're chipping away at it, Jake. That's the way cases are usually solved."

"Yeah, I know. The description sounds like the guy I've been seeing. Changing the subject, I have news for you, too." Jake described his conversation with Craig Thorpe's mom, including the death threats her daughter-in-law received. He also told her he was meeting Fletcher Patterson at 9:00. "Patterson didn't want to talk on the phone. He said he would tell me everything I wanted to know. That would be things like why he left the Bed and Breakfast before the explosion and more about the people loaning money to the Demirs. Also, about the other person leaving the B&B that Gladis says she saw. I'll ask him if he knows who that was, too. It should be an interesting conversation."

"It sounds like we have a few people with a motive for opening the valve on the gas line. The question is the means and opportunity. Who would know how to do it, and how would they get into the Bed and Breakfast to do it? It could have been any of the people staying there, but they would realize they could be caught in the explosion. It would be suicide. It's more likely either the accountant or this other guy who moved the valve. They would have the opportunity, and you wouldn't need to be an expert to move a valve. Be careful, Jake. Like I said before, if organized crime is involved, you don't want to get too close to it. The Fraud Unit hasn't had time to speak to Patterson yet. Did you say 9:00? I'll meet you at the building and go in with you."

"I can handle it, Dani. You're busy. Besides, I'm not sure Patterson wants to meet with a detective. I'll let you know as soon as I finish talking to him."

Dani's voice became firmer. "I'll meet you at 9:00, Jake."

The tone warned Jake she wouldn't be dissuaded, and that there was no point in trying. Jake gave her the address, and they hung up. He spent the next hour playing with Oliver.

The cat was lively, well, in an Oliver kind of way. He made a half-hearted lunging effort to catch a laser beam Jake traced across the floor. He'd been unsuccessful at catching the beam so many times that his efforts seemed to be to appease his owner. Jake often thought the cat's mind worked this way: Fool me once, joke's on you. Fool me twice, joke's on me. Fool me 1,000 times, it isn't a joke anymore.

Jake left the house at 8:40 p.m. to drive downtown for the meeting with Patterson. It pleased him that Dani wanted to join him. He had been apprehensive about meeting Patterson in that dingy warehouse/office. He parked in a vacant spot on Metcalfe Street. The downtown area was dead. A handful of people sauntered on Sparks in the humid night air. A young woman in a short skirt and beret posed with one leg forward, a wide smile and two fingers on each hand signaling a "V" as her companion snapped a photo. Jake approached the front entrance to the building to see Dani already there, leaning against the wall with her arms crossed and one leg bent at the knee with her foot braced against the bricks. She wore a light jacket and blue jeans. He waved at Dani as he approached and retrieved his phone and Patterson's business card from his pocket to make the call.

No answer.

He tried again with the same result.

"Well, that's strange," he said. "What should we do? Go for a beer and keep calling until he shows up?"

Dani removed her foot from the bricks and unfolded her arms. "The beer sounds good. Maybe he took off. It could be he decided talking to you would not be the best plan he came up with." She tried the glass door, but it rattled and remained in its locked position. She peered through the door to see a security guard sitting at a desk watching them.

Dani slid her badge from her jeans pocket and pressed it against the glass door. The security guard pulled himself from his chair with serious effort. The man had to be six feet six inches tall and 300 pounds, but he appeared to be in good shape. He wore dark pants with a white shirt and a name badge. A pair of new-looking, bright yellow running shoes completed his ensemble. His name tag identified him as Lucas, and he had crinkly, shoulder-length, fiery red hair and a goatee to match. Jake wondered if the color could be real. He lumbered toward Jake and Dani, examined her credentials, and unlocked the door.

"Help you?" Lucas said, his voice deep, as expected coming from that body. The perfect radio voice.

Dani said, "Maybe you can. We had a meeting with Fletcher Patterson. He's an accountant with Ottawa Independent Turkish Rugs on the second floor. We've called a few times, but he doesn't appear to be in. Do you know him? Have you seen him leave by any chance?"

"He should still be up there. Anybody leaving the building after 6:00 has to sign out. Maybe he was in the can when you called. Try again."

Jake dialed again but still no response.

Dani said, "We're worried he may be ill or something. It's not like him to miss a meeting."

The guard wasn't convinced. He glanced at Jake and then back at Dani. He held the door part way open. "Have a warrant?"

Dani flashed her best smile for Lucas. "Look, Lucas, maybe he didn't hear the phone. We don't want to *search* the place; we just want to see if he's there. We were supposed to have an important meeting; if you didn't see him leave, he must still be there. Let us in and we'll check."

Lucas thought for a minute, staring first at Dani, then at Jake, then back at Dani, clearly trying to decide what to do. Finally, he opened the door. He said, "Okay, but I'll have to go up with you." He locked the door behind them.

As the threesome walked to the elevator, Jake realized that someone could sneak past the guard when he made his rounds, so the sign-out system couldn't be that reliable. Lucas obviously took his job seriously, but Patterson could have slipped by him while he was away from his desk.

The elevator ground to a halt with a sigh on Patterson's floor, and the doors jerked open. Lucas towered over them as he led them to Patterson's office door. He knocked on the door. No response. He knocked harder. Still no response. He tried the door handle. It turned, and the door opened. He glanced over his shoulder at Dani and Jake with a concerned look. "What's the guy's name again?" he asked.

"Fletcher Patterson," Jake and Dani replied simultaneously.

Lucas called out, "Mr. Patterson. Are you here?"

No response.

Jake said, "He has an office in the back. I'll look for him there." Before the security guard could object, Jake parted the hanging rugs with a screech of the metal rings and shoved his way through. No sign of Patterson in the office.

Lucas stood in the doorway as Jake rounded the desk past the piles of papers. "I don't think you should do that. Patterson obviously isn't here."

Jake detected a hint of alcohol from Lucas's breath and wondered if it was from dinner or a flask in the security guard's drawer. Lord knows there would be boring hours to pass during the night.

"I just want to check something," Jake said. As soon as he was far enough around the desk, he looked at the security monitor. The snowy image gyrated on the screen, like the one he had seen on television sets years ago when the connection dropped. A rectangular space sat vacant where the laptop was when Jake visited the office last time.

Suddenly, Dani's muffled voice traveled through the hanging rugs in the showroom. "I think Patterson's here."

Jake and Lucas left the office and pushed their way through the hanging rugs, expecting to see Patterson standing in the showroom. Instead, they saw Dani in a corner, staring down at a pile of rolled rugs. She held her hand up and said, "Lucas, stay where you are."

But Lucas traipsed tentatively behind Jake until the two of them stood beside the pile of rolled rugs. He peered over Jake's shoulder to see what he and Dani were looking at. Jake heard Lucas gag seconds before the security guard stepped back and threw up all over his bright yellow runners.

CHAPTER THIRTY-ONE

DANI SWITCHED INTO detective mode like Superman donning his cape. All professional now, she examined the body, or at least what was visible. Only the blood-matted top of the man's head showed, but an indentation in his skull made it obvious he had been struck with something. She peeled back the rug so Jake could see his face. "Is this Patterson, Jake?"

Jake turned from handing Lucas a tissue and nodded. "Yes, it's the man I spoke to yesterday who said his name was Fletcher Patterson." He grimaced at the black and blue marks on the man's face. Angry, ragged red welts near the eyes differed from the bruises. Jake wondered what caused them.

Dani pulled out her phone and dialed 911, telling the dispatcher she was a detective and that she found a deceased man. She provided the address.

Lucas wiped his mouth as he tried to avoid looking at Patterson's body, but his eyes drifted between Dani, Jake, and the man rolled in the carpet. The security guard's face was as white as the ceramic pitcher at the Bed and Breakfast, and his grimace suggested he could be sick again at any moment. Jake moved to block his view. Dani suggested to Jake he should escort the security guard back downstairs, but Lucas shook his head.

"I'm fine," he said. "I'm sorry. It was just a shock."

Dani nodded. "I understand. You can go back to your desk. Don't leave until we talk to you, okay?"

Lucas nodded and practically ran from the showroom.

"What do you think?" Jake asked.

Dani shrugged. "Somebody might be trying to send a message to someone. It looks like someone tried to make him talk about something." She pointed to Patterson's face. "I expect those are burn marks. Where's the blood? This kind of beating would leave a trail of blood. Did the killer beat him somewhere else and bring him here? When the security guard has had time to recover, I'll ask him if he saw anyone entering or leaving. It wouldn't be hard for a single person to sneak past the security guard if he was on his rounds, though."

Jake nodded. *Exactly what I was thinking.* He said, "Patterson smoked like a chimney. They wouldn't have to go far for cigarettes if they burned him that way. That's what those marks look like. Patterson had a security monitor and laptop on his desk. Kind of like a nanny cam type thing. The image looked like a snowstorm when Lucas and I were just in there. The laptop is gone." He glanced toward the ceiling and pointed at the cameras in the corners. "The red light suggests the camera is on, but the image on the monitor just danced."

Dani said, "We'll see if we can recover anything from those cameras and search for other footage in the surrounding area. Maybe we'll get lucky. This has all the earmarks of organized crime, but maybe too much. Why wouldn't they just make Patterson disappear if they wanted him out of the way or if they were worried about him saying too much? Who would they be sending a message to? Was he meeting someone else here tonight? Did they want someone to find Patterson like this? Lots of questions."

Jake said nothing as Dani asked questions, but the more he thought about it, the more he agreed with Dani's assessment. As he contemplated what she said, a noise in the hall turned out to be the coroner arriving. Dani asked Jake to go downstairs to console the security guard while the coroner did his thing.

A cameraman started taking pictures of the crime scene, and officers strung yellow tape to secure the area as Jake left. He took the stairs and arrived at the security guard's desk to see that the man's face had regained some color. "Feeling better, Lucas?"

"I am, thanks. I'm embarrassed about throwing up like that. I've seen a lot of things but nothing like that."

Jake smelled the odor of alcohol again. He suspected Lucas took a nip when he returned to his desk. He said, "Don't worry about it, Lucas. I was a former investigative reporter, and I did the same thing when I saw my first body. A murder victim is not something anyone should see. I'm curious, though. Did anyone suspicious enter or leave the building at any time today?"

"No, but to be honest, I don't pay much attention during the day. People come and go all the time. As I mentioned, people sign in and out between six p.m. and six a.m. You can check the register." He pointed to an open book with a pen lying between in the crease centering the pages.

Jake ran his finger down the list of names, but none meant anything to him. Anybody who intended on torturing and killing Patterson wouldn't be using their own name, anyway. He knew Dani would investigate every name.

Jake glanced around. "What about security cameras? You must have cameras somewhere."

"Are you kidding? The owners of this building are too cheap to pay for cameras. Besides, if they had a camera, I would be out of a job, so I'm glad they don't. There might be some on the other side of the street, but you would be surprised how few there are. With the hit stores took from the pandemic, there's no spare cash to spend on cameras, and if they have one, it's aimed inside the store to catch shoplifters, not outside on the street."

Dani would check on that, too. Just as Jake thought of her, she appeared through the door leading to the stairs. She pulled Jake aside out of ear shot of the security guard. She held a plastic bag in her hand.

"We found the blood spatter all over the bathroom, so that's where they killed him. The coroner estimates time of death somewhere in the last few hours. With the beating Patterson took, it would have been noisy, so the fewer people around, the better for the killer."

Jake nodded. "I know you will question Lucas about security cameras, but I asked, and he didn't think there are many around. He said store owners can't afford them. I smelled alcohol on his breath though, upstairs, and down here. I'm not sure he's the most reliable witness."

"Okay, thanks." She glanced at the security guard, who regarded them intently. Wrinkles creased his forehead as he concentrated on their conversation. She lowered her voice and held up the bag. "We couldn't find a cell phone. The coroner found this in Patterson's pocket. I'd like you to take a picture of it and give it some thought. It might have something to do with you."

Jake glanced at Dani and frowned before turning to a wrinkled piece of paper inside the bag. It appeared to be a random string of letters and numbers. A password, perhaps?

He retrieved his phone from his pocket and snapped a picture. He enlarged the photo on his phone with his fingers and stared at the image.

JS184217419191720197209

"Could it be a password, Dani? What would it have to do with me?"

"It might be a password, Jake, but don't you think the first two letters are a weird coincidence? They could stand for Jake Scott."

CHAPTER THIRTY-TWO

JAKE ARRIVED HOME about two o'clock in the morning. The strange string of numbers occupied his mind all the way home. *What could it be?* Dani's intuition was usually not far off, but this time, she must be wrong. The "JS" at the front of the numbers was probably an integral part of the sequence. It could be a serial number for a new purchase that Patterson planned to register or an offshore account number. If the place acted as a front for money laundering, the latter could be the most likely explanation.

Jake set his phone on his nightstand in the bedroom, made sure Oliver had food and water, showered, and flopped into bed. He held his cell phone in front of his face and clicked the button to bring it to life. He stared at the picture of the numbers again, but a notification announcing a message distracted him. His phone had remained in his pocket since he took the picture of the numbers. He hadn't heard the phone ring or sensed its vibration, but the log indicated the call came around the time Dani found Patterson's body. When he called the number to retrieve the message, he learned it was from someone who said her name was Abigail Frost and that she would call back.

At first, Jake wrote the caller off as a scammer. Then he remembered the woman Willow's friend Julie Tremblay mentioned. Maybe it was her. He checked incoming calls to see if she had tried calling again, but only one showed up.

It took a while to fall asleep, and when he did, he tossed and turned, numbers flitting around in his head. At one point, he recalled in the morning, numbers marched through his head in single file, beating drums and blowing horns like a marching band. It seemed he wouldn't get much rest until the puzzle was resolved.

He woke to the sound of his phone ringing and bouncing on the bedside table, trying to vibrate itself onto the floor. The caller ID showed "unknown." He glanced at the clock, and as he did, it flipped over to 7:16 a.m. *Who would call at this ungodly hour?*

He lay back on his pillow with the phone to his ear and said, "Jake Scott."

The voice was female and sounded timid.

"Mr. Scott? This is Abigail Frost. Uh, I believe Julie Tremblay told you I might call."

Jake threw the covers aside, swung his feet off the bed, and sat on the edge. He rubbed his eyes with his free hand while attempting to shake the cobwebs fogging his brain.

"Yes, thank you for calling, Abigail. I assume Julie told you what my involvement is with Willow Altman. I was staying at the same Bed and Breakfast as Willow, and I feel like I need to help find out what happened. I'm helping a friend in the police department by gathering preliminary information. I must tell you, though, I can't keep anything I find out to myself. If it's noteworthy, I'm bound to pass the information along to the police. Are you okay with that?"

Abigail sighed. "Yes, everything has gone too far. Rivera needs to be stopped. I never met Willow, but we attended the same meetings, and we'd say hello in the halls. I heard she got mixed up with Dan Rivera. I should have warned her. I feel horrible for her family."

Jake said nothing.

Abigail continued. "Dan and I were involved for about a year. He treated me well at first and helped me with my career. We traveled to meetings together, and one thing led to another. I was naïve, and I believe now he took advantage of that. I didn't even know he was married for the longest time. He didn't tell me.

"Toward the end, he became more demanding. He became a different person. Wanting things done, like, yesterday. I don't know if his constituents became more demanding or what. It translated to our relationship. More demanding. Emotionally and physically. Anyway, I finally smartened up and decided our relationship wasn't going anywhere. I asked to meet him at his place to break it off. When I told him, he was furious."

Jake said quietly, "I understand he threatened to kill you."

"He went further than that. He put his hands around my neck and choked me until I saw stars. When he let go, I was gasping for air. He said we could stop seeing each other, but I had to find a new job. He left red welts on my neck. It was summer, and I had to wear turtleneck sweaters for a week until the marks went away enough that, with makeup, I could go back to my usual clothing. Thankfully, I knew of a vacancy and got a new job quickly away from Dan."

"That's terrible, Abigail. Rivera shouldn't be allowed to get away with this. As I said at the beginning, I might have to report this to the police, and I think they need to know what you've told me."

"Yes, I understand, and I agree. If you can, please warn me if the police are going to talk to Dan. I'll go into hiding for a while. But there's one more thing I must tell you before you talk to them."

"Okay, Abigail. The police will want to talk to you first before they speak to Dan. They'll need to corroborate your story. Please tell me everything."

"I want to tell you the main reason I feel bad about Willow. After Dan let me up, he warned me again not to tell anyone about our affair. He said that what he did was nothing. He said he had dangerous friends and seemed very proud of that." She hesitated before continuing. "If I said something before, Willow and all those other people might still be alive. He said he knew someone who could blow up my house and make it appear to be an accident."

CHAPTER THIRTY-THREE

JAKE SAT ON the edge of the bed, contemplating Abigail's revelations. Just when it seemed organized crime was the most likely suspect, a new wrinkle popped up. He thanked Abigail for being brave enough to come forward and promised to pass the information along to the police department. She seemed ready to cooperate and relieved to have told someone.

He wondered if Rivera really knew someone who could blow up a house or if it was just an idle threat. A threat of violence of any kind to be vindictive represented a complete lack of judgment at best, but to threaten to blow up somebody's house took everything to another level, especially under the circumstances. Jake realized this had gone way beyond him. Dani and her team would have to take over investigating Rivera. He shook his head at the way things piled up. Dani still had the murder in the Market to deal with, and the explosion of the Bed and Breakfast had become more and more complicated. He supposed this to be Dani's world. The one she lived in every day.

He rose from the bed and sauntered down the hall to his office in his pajamas. The bare hardwood floor chilled his bare feet. Oliver traipsed after him into the office. Jake added the newest information to his whiteboard, which looked more like caveman drawings. He just didn't want to forget anything.

A hunger pain jabbed at his stomach as he wrote, so when he finished, he retrieved his slippers and robe from the bedroom and wandered into the kitchen, where he cracked two eggs into the frying pan. He prepared his breakfast with his hands on autopilot while his mind whirled. He tried to assemble his thoughts for a call to Dani the minute he finished his breakfast.

But a different call interrupted his breakfast.

It was Avery's common-law husband, Nick, whose alarmed voice immediately sent shockwaves dancing through Jake. *Was there something wrong with Avery? Or the baby?*

"What is it, Nick? Is something wrong?"

"It's Avery, Jake. I'm calling from the hospital. Someone went through a stop sign and t-boned her car. The steering wheel airbag went off and knocked her unconscious for a few minutes. The paramedics took her by ambulance to the hospital, and I just arrived. I'm sitting beside her bed now. She was awake, but she has some memory loss. The doctors think it will be short term, but because of the pregnancy, they're keeping her for observation. She complained of a headache before she fell asleep. Her face is bruised, and the doctors think she has a concussion. They said she's lucky the airbag didn't break her nose."

The words spilled out of Jake's mouth like an avalanche. "Oh, my God, Nick. Are you sure she's okay? What about the baby? I'll come down right away."

"The doctors say she'll make a full recovery, but here's the thing, Jake. They need to do more tests regarding the baby. The doctor was wonderful at explaining everything, and there are risks. I'll tell you everything he said." Jake detected a quiver in Nick's voice. "The worst-case scenario is the fetus could have been harmed by the jolt. They'll perform tests for that. The doctor said they would wake Avery up and do a physical exam. There could also be longer-term effects if she experiences dizziness, nausea, or that kind of thing. It could interfere with prenatal care. It also could lead to preterm birth or a lower birth weight."

Jake's heart sank a little more with each word out of Nick's mouth. Each sentence carried with it a lead weight, pushing Jake further and further into the depths of despair.

Nick continued in a subdued tone. "The doctors are amazing here, and they're doing everything they can to help Avery, but it'll take time for them to determine whether there's a problem with the baby. As for you coming down, Jake, I suggest you hold off until we know what the outcome will be. Avery will need all the support she can get if the news is bad. It's up to you, of course, and you know you're welcome anytime, but my recommendation is that you come to Toronto when we know more. I would put Avery on the phone now, but she's still sleeping. I promise I'll call back and put her on later today. It might help with her memory if she talks to you."

Jake agreed with Nick's logic. Despite the shock of everything that happened to Avery, Nick remained level-headed. He liked Nick the first time Avery introduced them, and he really thought Avery found a keeper. Nick worked at a good job, had an outstanding personality and sense of humor, and most importantly, he thought the world of Avery. Jake knew Nick would do everything he could to help his daughter. His stomach churned from fear for his daughter and her baby, but he tried to sound stoic for his son-in-law, who would feel terrible.

"I agree, Nick. Please tell Avery you and I talked the minute she wakes up. I look forward to hearing from you later today. I'm sure she and the baby will be fine."

Jake rolled his eyes with his last statement. It was one of those things people say when they have no idea whether someone will be fine. He said it for his own peace of mind to convince himself that she would be fine.

They disconnected, and Jake set the phone on the kitchen table and sat staring unseeing for minutes. He barely noticed when Oliver jumped onto his lap and leaned into Jake before curling into a ball. The cat seemed to sense every time Jake needed comforting, and this was one of those times.

Any thoughts about the Bed and Breakfast explosion left his mind for the moment as he feared for Avery and the baby's safety. He never considered himself a religious man, but he said a brief prayer for them and for Nick. With his shoulders slumped, his body felt like all the energy had flown away. He looked down at Oliver and idly petted the cat, who responded with a deep, satisfied purr.

Jake said, "You know what, Oliver. No offense, but I need to talk to someone besides you. I need to call Dani."

CHAPTER THIRTY-FOUR

DANI SAT ACROSS from Jake at the kitchen table. Jake's phone call caught her on the way out the door to go to work, and she dropped in. It pleased Jake that she had taken time from her busy day to do that. They held hands as they talked in quiet tones, Jake in his pajamas and robe and Dami dressed for work.

They had spent the last half hour discussing Avery's situation, and relief washed over Jake with Dani's assurances. She had no way of knowing the severity of Avery's situation, of course, but she made the day seem brighter. Then, as it inevitably had to, the subject turned to the explosion. Jake had already decided to turn everything over to Dani and concentrate on Avery's situation, so he needed to bring her up to speed.

Dani said, "I sent the number sequence found on Patterson's body to the Fraud Unit. They're seeing if they can match it to offshore accounts or any other bank account. You haven't come up with any ideas, have you?"

"I thought about the numbers half the night. Even dreamed about it. These crazy numbers tramped through my head like a marching band. It was hilarious when I thought about it this morning. There's something else, though. I spoke with a woman called Abigail Frost. She had an affair with Dan Rivera, the MP, and she called me to talk about it. She called last night, but I didn't hear my phone. It was around the time you found Patterson's body, so we were kind of busy. She said he tried to choke her when she wanted to break off the relationship. But it was even more serious than that. Get this. He told her he knew someone who could blow up her house if she didn't keep quiet about the affair."

Dani's eyes never wavered from Jake's, nor did her expression change. It was like he told her there would be snow in the winter in Ottawa. She was the ultimate professional. She responded simply, "Okay, give me her contact information, and I'll assign a constable to follow up with her. We'll pay Dan Rivera a visit very soon. It could have been bravado, but we'll at least try to nail him with an assault charge if Abigail cooperates. It sounds like he deserves it. I really must get back to work, my dear. Tell me when you hear from Nick, okay?"

"I will, Dani. Thank you so much for stopping by."

They stood simultaneously and embraced. Jake held on for a little longer than usual, relishing in the comforting warmth of her body pressed against his. He wished she could stay longer but understood duty called.

Dani had one more thing to say before she left. "I would be happy to talk to Avery if you want, Jake. In fact, I want to. The most important thing for her, no matter what happens, is her emotional state. I can share some of my experience to help with that. In this job, we see all kinds of mental health issues, and my training helps. Let me know her condition and the best time to call."

"That would be amazing, Dani. She thinks a lot of you, and you can provide a perspective I can't, and Nick can't either." He snorted at the thought of him or Nick understanding much about pregnancy.

They kissed in the entrance, and Jake waved as she pulled out of the driveway. He watched her leave before shutting the door, sad to see her go. She influenced his life so much that he thought they should discuss making their relationship more permanent soon. Right now, though, many other things occupied their minds.

Jake showered and dressed in old shorts and a tee shirt. Still uncertain how to connect his phone to the printer, he sent the photo of the numbers to himself by email, which he opened on his computer, and printed the attachment, so he had it in front of him. He filled his time by undertaking various searches on the internet to figure out what the list of numbers could mean. He learned that the definition of a sequence is an ordered list of numbers that follows a pattern or rule. No logical pattern seemed to jump out of this set of numbers. If some rule applied, he didn't know what it would be. His last search revealed a list of mathematical problems that no one ever solved. *Now, that's encouraging.* If only Patterson hadn't attached the letters JS to the front of the numbers, he wouldn't have given them a second thought.

He tossed the page on the desk. Staring at it was getting him nowhere. It could be the combination for a safe, for all he knew. He walked from the office to the sunroom, where he sat in his lounge chair and pushed the lever back. The lever locked with a clunk as the footrest settled into a nice, comfortable position. He clicked the remote to turn on the television and found a mindless old movie he hoped to get lost in.

Jake had trouble concentrating as thoughts of Avery, Nick, and the baby collided in his head. He needed to fight off the "what-ifs." The TV blared away, but he paid little attention. The movie was about half over when his phone rang. It was Nick.

"Hi, Jake, I wanted tell you Avery's awake and talking." His voice sounded subdued. "I'm in the hall, so I need to keep my voice low. She can't recall anything about the accident, but she remembered me when she woke up, thank God. The doctor performed a physical examination and didn't detect any obvious problems with the fetus. She's hooked up to monitors to confirm the results. So far, everything is looking okay, but the concussion is still a worry. She said she wanted to talk to you when she woke up. Just a second, and I'll see if she's okay to speak with you. She's on sedatives, so she's pretty groggy."

Jake heard Nick's footsteps as he walked back to the room, followed by a rustling noise, which Jake assumed to be Nick handing the phone to Avery.

"Hel…Hello? Dad?" Jake's exuberance to talk to his daughter sank at the weakness in her voice. "Hi, Dad. They said I… they said I got in an accident. I don't remember. I'm scared, and I'm worried about the b… baby."

"Yes, sweetie, Nick said a car went through a red light and hit you, but don't worry. The doctors think the baby's going to be fine. You're in skilled hands at the hospital. They'll make sure everything is okay. There isn't a better place for you right now."

"Yeah. I don't even remem… uh, remember getting up this morning. I don't remember where I drove or what I ate for breakfast. I hope everything's going to be, uh, okay. My head is pounding, and I'm so tired." Her voice trailed off with the last few words.

"I'm sure everything will be fine, honey. I won't keep you on the phone. You can call me any time, and I'll stay in touch with Nick. Dani sends her love."

"Okay, love you, Dad. I…I think you should marry Dani."

Jake hesitated at Avery's words, but he said, "I love you too, sweetie."

Jake relaxed a little after speaking with Avery as he imagined the shuffling noise he heard again to be Nick taking the phone from her. Jake waited with the phone at his ear as footsteps preceded Nick's voice coming back on.

"She's asleep again, Jake. She'll be doing that a lot. Funny she mentioned that whole marriage thing at a time like that."

"I'm pretty sure sleep is the best thing she can do, Nick." Avery's comment about marriage took him aback, but he chose not to say anything.

"I agree. She mentioned that before her accident, you were almost caught in that explosion. How are *you* doing?"

"Ah, I'm doing fine. Dani asked me to do a little preliminary investigation, so I've been talking to people who knew the deceased. All the victims seem to have had secrets. We never know what will turn up when we dig."

"Are you getting anywhere?"

Jake sensed Nick wanted to spend a few minutes talking about something besides the accident, and it might be a pleasant break for him, too.

"I was supposed to meet the other survivor from the blast last night, but he wasn't available." Jake left out the fact he was dead. No point in alarming Nick, or it would be even worse if the news got back to Avery. "We found a note he apparently wrote." Jake read off the string of letters and numbers and mentioned the suggestion that the 'JS' at the front could refer to him.

"That's it? Nothing else? Weird. Do *you* think he meant the note for you?"

"I don't know, Nick. No idea. The letters at the front are the only reason to suggest it could have been for me. In fact, I didn't even notice. Dani pointed it out."

Nick rhymed off a few possibilities. "Password? Account number? Coded message?"

Jake hesitated. "We thought of the password and bank account number angles, and Dani's team is investigating them. But coded message? Do you mean a cipher? I don't think anyone thought of that. I know I didn't. It's possible, I suppose. It sounds very cloak-and-dagger-ish."

Nick chuckled. "Well, you know I like video games, Jake, and that was the first thing that popped into my head. Maybe he wanted to give you a message but didn't want it to be obvious to anyone else. I need to go, Jake, to be at Avery's bedside when she wakes up again."

"I understand. Thanks, Nick. Keep me posted. Oh, and Dani said she would be happy to talk to Avery when she's up to it. She has lots of experience with trauma as you can imagine."

They disconnected and Jake sat back in his chair, ruminating on Avery's comment about marriage. He suspected it was the drugs talking. He had feelings for Dani, but *marriage*? Whoa! That moved their relationship to a different level…so far, anyway. He pushed the idea from his head and wondered if the numbers really represented some kind of coded message to him.

Nick had introduced another avenue to explore.

CHAPTER THIRTY-FIVE

THE IDEA OF a coded message intrigued Jake but seemed to be a little "out there." *Why would anyone take the time to code a message for him? Why wouldn't Patterson just leave a message for him on his desk?* But then again, if the accountant worried about someone else seeing the message, it made some sense. Definitely intriguing.

He didn't want to interrupt Dani until later, so he spent the rest of the afternoon researching various cipher techniques online, from the relatively simple to the complex. He looked at the message again.

JS18421741919172019720099

What could it be?

Everything he tried turned the number sequence into even more gibberish. He was about to give up and call Dani to update her when she called.

"Hey, handsome. Any more news on Avery?"

"Hi, Dani. Yes, I spoke with her. She sounded groggy, but Nick said the doctors had her on sedatives. The doctors told him everything should turn out okay, but there's still a risk. I'm sure he'll call tonight with another update. He's a good young man, and he thinks the world of Avery." Jake left out Avery's marriage comment.

"That's a relief. So, what have you been up to? You're not just sitting around worrying, are you?"

"No, Nick brought something interesting to my attention when we talked. He suggested the number sequence could be a cipher of some kind, so I've been experimenting with various combinations. So far, all I've come up with is alphabet soup. How's it going with you?"

"That's an interesting premise. No news from my staff or the Fraud Division, so I guess they uncovered nothing so far. What are you doing this evening? I'm taking the night off, so a glass of wine might be in order. We could brainstorm on the case for a while. Maybe find something else to do after." A little throaty chuckle came over the line.

Jake's blood raced. "That sounds like a plan to me, Dani. I hadn't planned to go anywhere. I'll order something in. What are you inclined towards?"

"I haven't eaten Italian for a while. Well, okay, other than the pizza we had the other day. How about manicotti or chicken parmesan?"

"Great," Jake said, unsurprised Dani suggested Italian. He knew it to be a favorite. "I'll order so it will be here soon after you arrive. The wine is already in the refrigerator."

The call ended with Dani saying she was on her way out the door. Jake placed the order and changed from his ratty shorts and tee shirt into casual dress slacks and a white shirt. He left the shirt untucked and unbuttoned. When he checked himself out in the mirror, he thought she would approve.

A text from Emilie pinged on his phone. Unusually short and even more unusual because it was in complete sentences.

Hi J. Mom told me about Avery.
I hope she feels better soon.
See you soon.
E.

It gave Jake a great feeling that Emilie would be thoughtful enough to text him. He texted right back.

Thanks so much, Em.
Your thoughtfulness is very much appreciated.
I think she will be fine soon.
J.

Dani and the food delivery arrived at the same time. "It smells so good," she said as she followed Jake into the house after he paid the delivery man. "And I'm famished."

Jake said, "Em texted me saying she hoped Avery feels better soon. That's so special. You've raised your daughter right."

"Aw, I'm glad she did. I like to think I've raised her right. She can be a handful, but she's my handful. Reminds me of myself in my teenage years."

Dani pulled the dishes from the cupboard while Jake opened the wine bottle and poured two glasses of Cabernet Sauvignon. They sat at the table, chatting about Avery and enjoying each other's company. They toasted their future.

Dani looked amazing to Jake in the same yellow blouse and navy slacks she wore to work that morning, and he told her as they enjoyed their Italian food. "Why, thank you, dear," she said. "You look pretty good yourself. This is an old outfit, and I'm sure you've seen it before, but I appreciate the compliment. Changing the subject for the moment, I have my ideas about the explosion, but I'd like to hear your thoughts, Jake. You've been talking to all these people. What's your gut instinct?"

"I can say all the people kept secrets that may have driven them to do some bad things but murdering a bunch of people? I'm not sure about that. That makes me lean towards the organized crime angle."

"Okay," Dani said as she wiped her mouth with a napkin and picked up dishes from the table. "Let's clean up and move into your office. We'll put some things on your whiteboard."

Jake filled their glasses again and stowed the remaining dirty dishes in the dishwasher. He shuddered at the thought of the mess on his whiteboard.

As they walked to the office, Dani said, "I'm glad you don't keep the dishes in the stove anymore, Jake. That was just embarrassing."

"Okay, don't remind me. You don't know how much I cleaned up to fit them all in the cupboard. I guess you're an excellent influence on me."

They laughed as they entered the office.

Dani stopped a foot inside the door, staring at the scribbled words joined by squiggly lines on the whiteboard. "Oh, my gosh, Jake. What *is* that? A map of the traffic flow in Mexico City?"

"It's my attempt at a murder board," Jake said defensively. "I kind of jotted things down as I thought of them or as they came up."

Dani sat in Jake's chair. "Yeah, well, erase that. We'll start over. We have a giant board at the office that we've already started filling. What we do is start with 'what,' which is the explosion, of course. That would be in the middle. We place the people around the outside representing the 'who' and start linking everything together to come up with the 'why.' I'd like to try something different."

Jake snickered to himself at the comment about what now looked to him like doodles and did as Dani suggested. He stood with the dry erase pen poised upright in his hand, ready to write on the clean slate. He had felt drowsy from the effects of the wine, but now the excitement had energized him. This promised to be an interesting exercise.

Dani said, "Okay, let's look at each of the people that stayed at the B&B that night first. The Demirs, Thorpes, and Willow were there. Fletcher was there but left, and if we can trust our legally blind witness, we can add an unknown person who might have been there. Let's assume, for the sake of argument, that there was another person whom we'll call the mystery man. Any of them could have hired the mystery man. Oh, yes, we need to add Dan Rivera. He could've hired the man of mystery." Dani smirked. "We can eliminate you because you played pickleball until late. Let's write their names down on the left side of the board. Maybe we should add organized crime at the bottom. I don't know. Call it the Syndicate like they do on TV."

Jake wrote Omar Demir, Seda Demir, Craig Thorpe, Francis Thorpe, Willow Altman, Fletcher Patterson, Dan Rivera, Mystery Man, and Syndicate down the left side of the board as instructed.

"Okay, let's examine the means."

Jake wrote "Means" across the top.

Dani continued, "Any one of them could have moved the gas shut-off valve to the 'on' position. No tools necessary. No physical strength. No technical knowledge. We can put a check beside each of them." As Jake did that, Dani said, "Something just occurred to me. It's possible Fletcher and Mr. Mystery knew each other. Maybe draw a line between them with a question mark on it. You should draw a line linking the Syndicate to the Demirs, Patterson, and Mr. Mystery, too. The Syndicate would have the means through any of them. For that matter, Willow had the means, too, but I feel comfortable eliminating her as a suspect. Let's erase her from the list for now."

The new diagram already resembled the old one in Jake's mind after he drew a line connecting Fletcher and Mystery Man and another line up the left-hand side linking the Syndicate with the others, as Dani suggested. As he erased Willow from the list, he said, "We don't know what the igniter was. Something triggered the explosion."

"That's true, but I think it's fair to assume any of them could have set off some kind of ignition. The Fire Marshall confirmed any kind of spark can ignite gas, like a light switch, candle, match… Even static electricity. Taking something static out of the dryer could have set it off, but I can't see somebody doing that with the smell of gas lingering in the basement. Possibly somebody smelled the gas, went downstairs to check it out, turned on the light switch, and boom! Maybe the explosion happened before the murderer expected it to. We have to set the ignition aside for the moment."

Jake nodded in agreement.

Dani said, "Okay, now let's look at opportunity. How many of them had the opportunity to commit the crime?"

Jake said, "All of them except the Syndicate and Dan Rivera, but they had the opportunity through the others."

Dani nodded. "Yes, the ones who stayed there, for sure. The time stamp on the blurred images of Fletcher confirmed he could have opened the valve. He was there until just before the explosion. Our witness swears she saw Mr. Mystery just before the explosion, and the timing of her almost hitting you confirms it. *If* she actually saw someone leaving the Bed and Breakfast, he had the opportunity."

Jake placed a tick mark beside each of the names except the Syndicate. "What do we do with this one?" he asked as he tapped on it with the end of the pen.

"Draw a line between it and the others like you did before."

Jake did as she said and stepped back, admiring his handiwork. He glanced at Dani. "Okay, what do we have?"

"Not much yet, Jake. The only ones not linked to anyone else so far are the Thorpes and Willow." She set her empty wine glass on the desk and stared at the board with her chin on her palm, tapping her cheek with her finger.

"Care for a top-up, Dani?" Jake asked.

"Uh, yes, that sounds good, thanks," Dani said. "I'm glad you write small so there's space left on the board. We need to talk about motives now."

CHAPTER THIRTY-SIX

JAKE RETURNED FROM the kitchen with two glasses of wine. He turned the corner to see Dani still gazing at the whiteboard. She glanced up, smiling when he arrived.

"I was just thinking," he said as he retrieved the pen from the desk. "There's someone we didn't put on the board. That's the father of Willow's baby. He's another 'unknown,' but he's a possibility."

"Yes, that's true. He's on the board at the office, but I forgot about him tonight. We need to find out who he is and what kind of guy he is. You better add him to the list. We haven't established any connection between him and the others yet, but he would have the same means as the rest."

Jake added "Baby Dad" to the end of the list with a question mark under "Opportunity." He agreed with Dani he would need some connection to a person on the list to have been involved in the explosion unless...

"Do you think the baby dad could have snuck in and out with no one knowing? Maybe he's the mystery man. It was a dark night. The security cameras in the neighborhood might as well not exist."

"Our tech team has scoured the neighborhood security cameras and cleaned up the images as much as possible. There's the image of the hunched over man we're almost certain was Patterson. We're still unsure if the man the old lady, Gladis, talked about came from the B&B, but it's possible. There are video images of a handful of blurred random people on the sidewalk at night, and my team is trying to clear up those pictures. Let's leave the list of suspects as is. If we eliminate them, we'll figure out someone else who might've snuck into the house. Our list is long enough as it is."

Dani took a sip of her wine. She said, "This wine is going down well tonight. I can't remember the last time I relaxed in the evening. By the way, we've identified the stabber from the Market incident. It wasn't Shrek or Brad Pitt as the witnesses described him. Just another person who ruined his life in a moment of extremely bad judgment. We just need to find him now." She laughed abruptly, prompting Jake to glance at her with a frown.

"Sorry, I just realized I said I'm relaxing, and here we are talking about my cases. We're talking about work, and yet, I feel relaxed! There's a difference, though. I'm discussing the case with you, and that relaxes me. I hope you don't mind that we're doing this, Jake. I promise I don't always bring my work home."

"Of course, I don't, Dani. I'm enjoying this, and I'm learning things at the same time. I just love spending time with you."

Dani stood and hugged Jake tightly, her face flushed from the wine. Jake had to be careful not to leave a mark on the back of her blouse with the pen as he returned the hug. She pulled back and said, "Shall we finish this and move on to something more pleasant?"

Jake agreed, and Dani sat on the chair again.

"Okay, let's look at motive, starting with the Demirs. According to Patterson, the Demirs owed serious people a lot of money. That could be a motive. Did the Demirs try to get rid of Patterson? Or Gladis's mystery man could have been engaged by the Syndicate to kill Patterson and the Demirs. Doubtful anyone else at the B&B would have it in for the Demirs. The Demirs were involved in a front to launder money, apparently, with their rug business, so that points to Patterson and the mystery man with motive. Like you said, the mystery man could've been the baby dad, too."

Jake wrote Dani's theories under motive. A thought occurred to him as Dani spoke. "What about murder/suicide? Could the Demirs have been in so deep that they took the only way out they could think of?"

Dani nodded. "It's possible, Jake, but why take the Thorpes and Willow with them? One could make a case for trying to take out Patterson to pay him back for threatening to expose them. Maybe they panicked when he told them he knew what was going on. We can't rule anything out, so I agree you should add murder/suicide under the motive column beside their names. Maybe they wanted to get rid of Patterson, but things went wrong. Add Patterson as a possible motive for the Demirs, too."

Jake wrote, and Dani moved on. "What about Craig and Francis Thorpe? You said Craig was in Special Forces, but that wouldn't give him a reason to kill anybody at the Bed and Breakfast. It might give someone a reason to kill him if they brought the war to our shores. What if our mystery man came to Canada looking for revenge for something Craig did overseas? I suppose the same logic could apply to anyone staying at the B&B. If Mr. Mystery carried a grudge against any of the residents, he might have motive." Dani shook her head, frustrated she didn't know the identity of the mystery man, if he even existed. "I don't think Craig has a motive that we can pinpoint yet, do you?"

Jake left the space blank but said, "Unless he wanted to get rid of Francis. It seemed like the marriage was on the rocks. Maybe he used the explosion to cover up getting rid of her without raising suspicion. Maybe there was an insurance policy that someone in Craig's life could benefit from. His mom, maybe?"

"Wow, you've got a devious mind. Good thinking, Jake. I'll ask my team to investigate Craig's affairs to see if they can dig up anything to suggest he wanted to get rid of Francis on a permanent basis. Write Francis and insurance as a motive for Craig."

Jake wrote and then strode to the desk and consulted the notes he had taken from his discussion with Thorpe's mother. "Craig's mom said he had PTSD, and he wanted a divorce. It sounded like things got ugly between him and Francis. His mother said his personality changed with his PTSD. What if he snapped? From his career in the Special Forces, he could very well have the knowledge to set off a gas explosion, although we agreed it didn't require any special training. Should we put murder/suicide beside Craig's name?"

"Yes, we should, Jake." She laughed. "You might have to write on the wall if this keeps up. You might have a paint job to do when this is over. What about Francis? Any thoughts on her?"

"It just seems like she was a horrible person. I don't know that she would have any motive. Do you?"

"No, let's leave her for now. What about Willow?"

"We already took her off the board. Willow just seemed to be a naïve person a predator took advantage of."

"I agree. Let's leave her for now, too. Now, we're down to Fletcher Patterson. What are your thoughts on him?"

"He had lots of motive, Dani. He said it upset him that the Demirs duped him for years. But how could he not have known? He did their books. He threatened to expose them. He wanted to tell me something. Maybe that was it. Maybe he wanted to confess. Or it was his way of hitting back at the organized crime group that controlled the Demirs. He's a good possibility. Why did he go back to the Bed and Breakfast at night? He said the Demirs told him they would talk to him after breakfast. He left, but why go back? Someone could have hired him to do it. Maybe he was closer to organized crime than we thought. And who killed him? Someone who thought he knew too much? Then there's the message he may or may not have left for me. He's dead now, and we don't have answers to any of those questions."

"Well, if he did it, Jake, we would have to determine his motive. Can you summarize all that on the board?"

With Dani's helpful suggestions, Jake crammed it all in and left room for what was to come.

They went on like this for the Syndicate, the mystery man, and the baby's father. As they brainstormed ideas, Jake's writing became smaller and smaller on the board. When they got to the mystery man, Jake filled the board with several possibilities.

When Jake finished writing, they stood back and examined their handiwork.

Someone could've hired Patterson, or he took it upon himself to rid the world of the Demirs.

Someone could've hired Mr. Mystery to get rid of the Demirs and, possibly, Patterson or Willow.

Either of the Thorpes may have wanted to kill the other or have done it for insurance purposes.

Craig Thorpe could have snapped.

Dan Rivera may have hired Mr. Mystery to kill Willow.

The baby's father may have hired Mr. Mystery to kill Willow.

Jake sat on a blue exercise ball he kept in the office, mostly to keep it out of the way. He couldn't remember the last time he used it for its intended purpose. He looked at the board and laughed as he flipped the marker into the air and caught it. "How do we sort through all this, Dani? It seems like the most likely candidate is Mr. Mystery, although I wouldn't rule out Patterson. The burning question is, who would take out a house full of people unless someone hired them? It would have to be someone desperate or who didn't care, like organized crime." He glanced at Thorpe's name. "Or someone who snapped."

Dani stared at the board. Jake could almost see the wheels grinding as she analyzed everything Jake had written. It seemed like the board barely held itself on the wall under the weight of the words and lines.

Finally, Dani said, "I agree it's possible, Jake, but the message Patterson had in his pocket bothers me. It's like you said, who would want to take out an entire house full of people? I agree organized crime might do that. We're missing two crucial pieces of information. We need to know if Mr. Mystery was at the house that night, and we need to understand the message."

CHAPTER THIRTY-SEVEN

IT DIDN'T SURPRISE Jake when Dani announced she needed to go home to rest. Disappointed maybe but not surprised. They had brainstormed for two hours and finished a bottle of wine. That, on top of Dani's ridiculous crime-solving hours at work, wore on her. He saw the dark pouches under her eyes. She looked exhausted.

"It's okay, Dani," Jake said when she apologized over and over. "If I can help with this case, I will. The sooner you can put this case to rest, the better."

"I know. It just seems we're inundated right now. We'll get through."

They embraced and kissed at the door, and Jake stood in the entrance as she climbed into her car. A dent on the passenger door of her silver Hyundai Tucson drew his attention. He hadn't noticed it before. He wondered if the new driver, Emilie, or speed demon Dani put it there. Either could be possible suspects. She acknowledged his wave as she peeled out of the driveway and into the night back to her condo. Jake smiled to himself at the speedy Dani. No one would ever accuse her of holding up traffic.

He was about to close the door when a dark car approached from the opposite direction at low speed. It met Dani's car about halfway down the street. Compared to Dani's speed, the approaching car practically idled. A shiver slithered along Jake's spine as the driver turned towards him in the open doorway. The hall lights behind him lit him up like an actor in the spotlight onstage. The driver and Jake locked eyes as the dark car drove by and continued down the street. A sliver of recognition.

Jake shut the door and frowned. *Why did he react like that?* His hands shook as he stashed the empty wine bottle into the recyclable bin and the dirty glasses into the dishwasher. He didn't have to ask himself why. He knew. The car and its driver reminded him of the vehicle in the parking lot at the hotel. He sensed the driver watched him then, and this person seemed to drive too slowly and was watching him now.

He had a talk with himself. *I'm just being paranoid.* The city installed a traffic calming bump farther down the street when younger parents with kids complained about speeding cars. *Everyone* slowed down in front of his house now. Dani could have been one of the speeding cars residents complained about. He told himself the driver was just a nosy neighbor, that he would never see the car again. But, if he did, he resolved to pay more attention to the car and less to the driver. Here he was an experienced investigative reporter, and all he could do was describe the car as big and dark. Ridiculous! Next time, if there was a next time, he promised himself to write down the license plate number. It would be easy enough for Dani's team to run the plate and confirm it meant nothing.

He plunked down in the chair with drowsiness overcoming him. The effects of the wine, he guessed, and he and Dani had spent a lot of time brainstorming about the explosion. He had to admit it became a tiring exercise. And he also agreed with Dani that they were missing something. He resolved to research the string of numbers more in the morning.

Oliver wandered into the room and jumped onto his lap to keep him company. As Jake's eyelids grew heavy, his phone rang. A disgruntled Oliver thumped down to the floor again with a throaty disapproving growl when Jake sat up to answer the call. Not surprisingly, Dani wanted to reiterate how much she enjoyed the evening. She said, "I ran through the shower, and I'm ready for bed. How about you?"

Jake thought of the dark car but kept it to himself. Dani had enough on her mind. "I dozed off in my chair. The wine and all that deep analysis affected both of us, I guess. I hope you sleep well, Dani."

They said their good nights, and Jake got ready for bed. He climbed under the covers and reached to shut off the bedside lamp when his phone rang again. *Dani can't sleep.*

But it wasn't Dani. It was Nick, and his voice sounded subdued and almost tearful.

"I wanted to let you know, Jake, that Avery took a turn for the worse about an hour ago. Her headaches became much more severe, and she threw up. The doctors said it could be a brain bleed. They're doing some imaging now and, depending on the results, will operate soon. They kicked me out of the room, so I don't know what's going on now."

The news shocked Jake into silence. Images co-mingled in his head. He almost offered the usual false assurances that everything would be okay, but how could he say that? He said instead, "There's nothing we can do, Nick. As you said before, she's in the best hands possible, so they'll do what they have to do. You must stay strong for Avery, and I know you will."

Nick's voice rose as he said, "I don't want to lose her or the baby, Jake."

"Of course, Nick. Let's stay calm and wait for the doctors to do their job. Call me as soon as you hear something. It doesn't matter what time, okay? My phone will be on."

They talked a while longer. Nick seemed to need to talk, and perhaps Jake did, too. They both seemed to perk up, the more they talked. When they disconnected, Jake sat back on the pillows against the headboard in an upright position. The bedside lamp still cast deep shadows around the room. His eyes closed for a minute, but it was as if a trap ensnared him, and he couldn't extract himself. Powerless to do anything.

His eyes snapped open again.

Another glass of wine beckoned, but he doubted it would help, so he settled under the covers, pulling them to his eyes. Shutting his mind off would be impossible. His thoughts whirled with a kaleidoscope of imagery about the activity around his daughter at the hospital in Toronto. The state of the deteriorating health-care system worried him, but he convinced himself his daughter's condition would be serious enough to attract the attention needed. He repeatedly told himself that everything would be okay, that the doctors were experts in their field. Nope, he decided, he had to go to Toronto to be with his daughter. He wouldn't sleep well until the call came from Nick, but his body disagreed, and he drifted into an unsettled slumber.

CHAPTER THIRTY-EIGHT

JAKE GUESSED HE fell into a deep sleep around five a.m. At least that was the last time of many he turned over to glimpse the numbers on the clock. He remembered nothing after until the phone vibrated on his nightstand, startling him. Light seeped in at the edges of the blind, but the room remained dark by his bed, and he fumbled around until he brushed the phone off the nightstand. Oliver lifted his head from the foot of the bed to identify the source of the commotion. Jake peeled back the covers to retrieve the phone from the floor. He squinted as the brilliant screen lit when he pressed the button on the side. He saw Nick's name and number.

"Hi, Jake," Nick said. "I didn't want to disturb you last night because I didn't know much until this morning. They wheeled Avery into surgery a few minutes ago. The doctors confirmed a brain bleed from the concussion. They're saying now the concussion must've been worse than they had hoped at first." Nick drew in a deep breath. "They also said it's a delicate surgery, so they won't have a definitive answer about either Avery or the baby until they're finished. It will take a few hours, Jake."

"Okay, Nick, thanks for keeping me posted. Are you sure you don't want me to come down?"

"I think you should wait, Jake. We can't do anything but wait. Stay busy, and we'll sort things out once we know the status. I went to the collision center yesterday and retrieved her stuff. Her car's a write-off. We're all lucky she wasn't killed. The accident caved in the whole passenger side. The other driver hit her at the passenger door. He was unharmed."

Jake perceived how deflated Nick's voice sounded, but the young man's parents lived in Toronto and would console him. He must not have slept much, either. Jake did his best to sound reassuring, although not reassured himself. "I'm confident the doctors are experts at what they do. Let's leave everything in their hands, Nick, and trust what they do. Try to get some rest and please call as soon as you hear something. My phone will always be on."

Jake remained torn when he got off the phone. Nick was right that there was nothing either of them could do until Avery came out of surgery, but he desperately wanted to be close when his baby girl woke up. He recalled that he and Mia agreed on many things, one of which was that they would raise their daughter to be independent. Avery picked a man in Nick who was raised the same way. Sometimes, being the parent of an adult child offered challenges, but he concluded again he would stay in Ottawa until Nick and Avery needed him in Toronto. Or at least for a day or two more.

As he sat on the edge of the bed in his pajamas, Jake glanced at the clock and decided Dani would be up in a few minutes to prepare for work. He needed to talk to her. He showered to clear his head, pulled on shorts and a tee shirt, and called. She answered right away with a nervous question.

"Any word on Avery?"

Jake explained what Nick had told him, and Dani did her best to reassure him. There really wasn't anything to be said. Everyone had to wait. They didn't talk about the case at all. Too many more important things on both of their minds.

When they hung up, Jake trudged to the kitchen to prepare breakfast. He glanced sideways at the whiteboard on the way by his office. Barely any white remained visible through the squiggles. With Avery still on his mind, he remembered how rapidly the time had passed when he and Dani analyzed the explosion and the people involved. She was so easy to talk to. He was relaxed, and they accomplished so much, including polishing off a bottle of wine. It was a special evening, even if they just worked on solving a crime.

He didn't feel at all hungry but knew he should eat something, so he dropped two pieces of rye bread in the toaster. He filled Oliver's bowls with cat food and water. Then he ground beans to get the coffee started. It occurred to him that the newspaper should have been delivered by now, so he wandered to the front door to check. An elastic band encircled the rolled-up paper out of reach on the porch.

The morning ritual with the new carrier involved removing the elastic band, unrolling the newspaper, and rolling it back up in the opposite direction to flatten it enough to read it. He guessed the carrier found it easier to throw rolled up, but finding the newspaper in the form of a cylinder wrapped in an elastic band every morning annoyed him. In his day, paper carriers didn't drive. Kids lugged the papers in a bag or hauled them in a wagon and delivered them right to the doorstep, and the papers had more content and included flyers, so they weighed more. As he stepped out to pick up the paper on the overcast day, he guessed his annoyance this morning had more to do with his concern for Avery. Unbeknownst to the paper carrier, he became the foil for Jake's frustration.

Jake's toast popped up as he flattened the newspaper. Once he slathered butter and peanut butter on his toast, completed the flattening ritual, and poured his coffee, he settled down for breakfast. He munched on the toast and flipped through the newspaper until he came to the obituary section. He scanned through the names and found an obit for Fletcher Patterson.

The writeup was sparse, mentioning a couple of family members living out of town and that he was born in Toronto. Whoever wrote the obituary either didn't know him well or didn't care. Jake thought it was sad when someone's life ended that way, but he guessed it depended on how you lived it.

The short obituary mentioned the time and date of the funeral. Jake glanced at his watch. Today at 10:00. He read the obituary again and decided to attend, at least the internment. He didn't know why but suspected it was because Patterson wanted to talk to him and ended up dead the night of the proposed meeting. Jake felt somehow at least a little responsible.

Based on the size of the obituary, likely only a few would show up. One more in the crowd wouldn't hurt. The time on his watch suggested he needed to hurry to make the funeral on time. He didn't want to miss a call from Nick, but he also didn't want to sit around the house waiting. *Waiting's the worst.*

He wolfed down the rest of his breakfast and changed into a blue dress shirt with gray slacks. The drive to the funeral home in the east end took about twenty-five minutes. Plenty of parking remained beside the building. He sat in the back of the funeral home behind about twenty people. The funeral was short with no one offering anecdotes about Patterson's life despite being asked. The Minister offered a few generic comments, and it ended. If Patterson's picture hadn't been on a table at the front, it would have been difficult to tell whose funeral it was.

When it ended, a few attendees glanced curiously at Jake on the way out. He followed the crowd on foot on a path up a hill until the mourners reached the spot of Patterson's interment. The Minister offered a few words, and the coffin was lowered into Patterson's ultimate resting place. A couple of mourners tossed flowers onto the coffin. Quick but respectful.

As Jake turned to return down the path to the parking lot, a vehicle passed slowly on the other side of the cars lining the driveway. Too many cars sat between Jake and the passing car to see the driver or the license plate, but the familiar crawling sensation crept along his spine. The car was big and dark. Jake hustled between two parked cars to glimpse the plate, but the car sped up and turned the corner. It looked to Jake like the same car he had seen several times already.

CHAPTER THIRTY-NINE

JAKE STARED AS the car raced around the corner. This had to be more than a coincidence. He acknowledged the potential for thousands of dark cars in a city of a million people, and he still hadn't been able to identify the make or the license number. He had to admit he still didn't know if he was being paranoid. Maybe the driver picked someone up at the funeral or dropped someone off to visit a gravesite. It was impossible to tell through the darkened windows if the driver was alone. Jake asked himself why anyone would track him. He didn't come up with an answer.

He turned to continue down the pathway when his phone rang. It was Dani.

"Just checking in to make sure you're doing okay and ask if you've heard anything from Nick."

"Not yet. I'm doing okay, thanks, Dani. Waiting is hard, but I'm sure he'll call the minute the surgery is over," Jake said as a handful of mourners passed, chattering among themselves on the path.

"It sounds like you're out and about, at least."

"Yeah. I noticed in the paper it was Fletcher Patterson's funeral today, so I attended."

Silence.

Jake continued to walk toward his car in the parking lot. "About twenty people attended. Kind of sad, really. I mean, any funeral is sad, but you would think he would have had *some* friends. He was born in Toronto, but I didn't see any cameras broadcasting live, and there was no mention of an online viewing of the funeral in the obit."

Dani said, "Why go, Jake? Don't you have enough going on without attending a funeral for some guy you met, what, once?"

"I don't know, Dani. I feel kind of bad that he died the night we were supposed to meet. I just felt compelled to go. Besides, I didn't want to stay in the house by myself waiting for Nick's phone call."

"Well, you could have gone to the mall to be around people and bought an ice cream or something. Anyway, speaking of Patterson, the coroner's report came in. He confirmed the marks on Patterson's face as cigarette burns. Whoever killed him tried to exact some kind of revenge or extract information. Marks on his wrists suggest he had been tied up, probably in the bathroom stall.

"The blow to the head wasn't the cause of death. The attacker probably wanted to stun him before taking him to the bathroom. Forensics found traces of blood and scrape marks on the floor in two directions. The investigators found a rag in the bathroom covered in what turned out to be Patterson's saliva, so the perp likely stuffed it in his mouth to keep the noise down. A six-inch blade to the heart caused the fatal wound. The perpetrator knew what he was doing. We haven't found the murder weapon. I seem to get more than my share of stabbings lately. The one in the Market and now this. Oh, and by the way, there were no fingerprints anywhere at the scene. Whoever did it wiped the crime scene clean. The investigators confirmed there was no cell phone."

Jake reached his car, held the phone in his left hand while he clicked the key fob with the other hand, and climbed in. "That's awful that someone tortured him. I wonder what they wanted. Wait, you're not connecting this to the stabbing in the Market, are you?"

"No, I'm not suggesting that, Jake. I just meant my hands are full with stabbings. The way the perpetrator inflicted the wound and applied the cigarette suggests a professional hit. You need to be vigilant, Jake. Be careful who you talk to. In fact, maybe you should back off completely. You have enough on your mind with Avery. You've been an immense help, but it's time to stand down."

"I think the same dark car drove by again, Dani. The one that was at the hotel. You met it last night when you left my place, and one just like it drove by the internment just now. I can't be sure. I can't give you a make or model or a license plate. It gives me the creeps every time I see a black or dark navy car. You must think I'm nuts."

"Not at all, Jake. Your intuition is great. If you see it again, try to get a plate we can run through the system. I'll ask one of my constables to circle through your neighborhood periodically to see if they can spot anything unusual. If he's tracking you, he may park his car a block down the street, although he doesn't seem to care if you spot him. Maybe someone is trying to scare you off without being too obvious. Leave the case alone, Jake. Promise?"

"Yes, Dani, I promise."

They chatted for a few more minutes until Jake's phone buzzed, announcing another call. "I have to go, Dani. Another call is coming in, and it could be from Nick."

"Okay, be careful, Jake."

He didn't recognize the number or the voice that came on the phone, although it sounded familiar. She introduced herself as Craig Thorpe's mother.

"Hello, Mrs. Thorpe. It's good to hear from you. I hope you're doing alright."

"Hello, Mr. Scott. I hope I'm not bothering you." She didn't wait for an answer. "Have you or your friends at the police department made any progress investigating the explosion? No one has contacted me yet."

"The police department is doing everything they can, Mrs. Thorpe. They need time to investigate the leads since multiple people were involved. I'm sure someone will be in touch soon."

"Okay. Since the police department hasn't contacted me, I thought I should pass some information on to you. You seem to be connected to them, and I hope you will pass along the information as soon as possible. It's important."

"Sure, Mrs. Thorpe, what do you want me to pass along?"

"I didn't tell you everything when we talked. To be honest, I forgot. I was in such a state. I spoke with Craig about a week before the explosion. Remember, I told you he wanted a divorce? He told me he needed to change his will. I'm the executor of his estate, so he wanted to make sure I was aware. I spoke with his lawyer this morning, and he told me Craig had scheduled a meeting with him for this week. The lawyer showed me the will, and it hadn't been changed. It still left all his possessions to his witch of a wife, Francis."

"Forgive me for asking, Mrs. Thorpe, but did Craig have a lot of money?"

"Not that I know of, but I know of an insurance policy with her as the beneficiary. Why, I'll never know. I don't know what he saw in that woman. She needed serious help. She met with a psychologist after she pretended to be a nurse and killed that person, but she needed a lot more than that."

"I'm sure the police department will investigate it. You seem convinced that Francis was involved, but why kill herself, too? It seems like an awful price to pay just because Craig wanted a divorce."

"I'm telling you she was *crazy*, Mr. Scott."

"Okay, thank you for letting me know, Mrs. Thorpe. I'll pass the information along to my friend at the police department."

When Jake got off the phone, he sat in his car, reflecting on what Mrs. Thorpe said. It was possible that Francis decided if she couldn't have Craig, no one else would either. But there was another possibility. If she was as crazy as Mrs. Thorpe said, the possibility existed that she miscalculated how quickly the explosion would happen. Maybe she wasn't crazy enough to kill herself but enough to kill Craig and a bunch of people with him. Just made a mistake and killed herself, too. He wondered if Dani and her staff would ever figure this enigma out.

CHAPTER FORTY

JAKE USED HIS car's hands-free feature to dial Dani on the way home. Avery's deliberate instructions helped him muddle through connecting it. She and Nick insisted on dragging Jake into the 21st century, and he was sometimes glad they persisted. This was one of those times. He explained everything Mrs. Thorpe had told him about the insurance policy to Dani.

"Funny you should mention the insurance policy, Jake. After our discussion last night, I asked one of my constables to check for insurance policies in Craig Thorpe's name. Guess what? The term life policy with Francis as the beneficiary had a value of half a million dollars. I confirmed he didn't change the beneficiary. It could be a motive for murder, but why kill yourself at the same time? It makes no sense."

Jake pumped the brakes at a green light as a car sailed through the intersection on his right on red. "Oh, my God. A car just ran a red light. He would have creamed me if I hadn't been paying attention." Thoughts of Avery and her accident invaded his mind. He wished Nick would call.

"I've been reflecting on Francis, Dani. There are two explanations that I can think of. One is the old lover's thing of if I can't have him, nobody can. Mrs. Thorpe believes Francis was mentally ill, so that's possible. But here's another theory. They found Willow in the basement, right? What if Francis turned on the gas and was about to leave when Willow smelled something and wandered downstairs to check on where the odor was coming from? Maybe something or someone delayed Francis from leaving. Willow could have turned on the light in the laundry room, which caused enough sparks to set off the gas buildup, and that would be it. Francis's plan might have been to say she just went out for some fresh air or to the store for something when the explosion happened."

Jake's phone dinged, announcing the arrival of a text.

"It's an excellent theory, Jake, but why would Willow go downstairs? Wouldn't she ask the owners to check? And your theory doesn't explain why someone tortured Patterson, but maybe there's no connection between the two things. I mean, between Patterson's murder and the B&B blowing up. The Fraud Unit is continuing to investigate the organized crime angle and the Demirs and Patterson's involvement. I'm waiting to find out what they discover.

"Francis's estate will benefit from the will and the insurance policy now. I wonder who benefits from the estate. Maybe we're looking at this all wrong, Jake. Could it be someone connected to Francis or Francis herself who hired Fletcher or the mystery man to set off the explosion? We don't know how the mystery man got into the house… if he did. Patterson certainly accessed the house. He seems like the most likely one to have caused the explosion." Dani sighed. "I keep going back and forth between Mr. Mystery and Patterson. Looks like we need to explore the estate angle, too."

Jake arrived at his house and pressed the button for the garage door opener. He drove his car into the garage, but Dani's voice broke up, so he backed out.

"…member what I said, Jake. For the last time, it's time to step away from the investigation. I'm not very convincing. I ask you to step away and then discuss it with you. If you hear anything more, I know you'll pass it along, but you need to put all your energy into helping your daughter now. Have you made plans to go down yet?"

"Not yet, Dani. I'm waiting for the call from Nick, and then I'll make plans to go. I'm expecting him to call any minute."

They finished their conversation, and Jake pulled back into the garage, pressing the button to close the door behind him. He checked the text to see Nick planned to call him soon with an update. Oliver greeted him at the door by winding through Jake's legs and purring softly. A glance at his watch told Jake it was early afternoon. Based on his fatigue level, it seemed closer to midnight. The lack of sleep last night and the activity today exhausted him. He decided he needed to lie down for a nap.

He no sooner closed his eyes than the phone rang again. The clock showed him his nap lasted about ten minutes. His head felt a size bigger, as he shook the grogginess away.

Nick's subdued voice came on the line.

"Hi, Jake, Avery's finally out of surgery. The doctor just told me. Sorry, I didn't get back to you sooner. I fell asleep in the visitor's area here. Anyway, the doctor said the surgery went well. They're not letting me see her yet. They say she's stable, and they will have a better idea when she wakes up and they're able to do some cognitive tests."

Cognitive tests? Jake asked himself. *Are they worried she will have memory issues?*

Nick continued. "Apparently, there can be brain damage from a bleed, so they need to do more tests. The doctor said the baby seems to be okay. He said we'll have to wait a couple of days before they can say definitively."

Each word pummeled Jake. *How am I going to survive a couple of days sitting here waiting and wondering?* But he said, "Thanks for calling, Nick. I'll plan to come down in two days. I'll take the train and Uber from the station to your place. I promise I won't be a nuisance while I'm there, but I need to see my daughter for myself. I'm sure she'll be alright." There it was. The false promise he tried to avoid. He couldn't think of anything else to say.

"That would be great if you come down then, Jake. I understand you need to see her, and of course, you won't be a nuisance. I'm confident she'll be alright, too. She's strong. She'll come out of this. So will the baby. We just have to be patient."

Now Nick was supporting him, Jake thought. The two of them took turns supporting each other, and he was grateful.

"By the way," Nick asked. "How's that case going? Did you solve the cipher?"

"I haven't even had time to look at it," Jake said ruefully. "There's so much going on with the case and Avery. Now Dani thinks I should stay away from investigating. She wants me to focus on Avery, and she's right. That's what I need to do."

"Well, I've had a lot of time to brood during the last few hours, and if you intend to examine the numbers again, I suggest the simpler the formula, the better. If the guy, what's his name, really wanted to leave you a message that would be incomprehensible to his enemies but easy for you, he wouldn't use some complicated formula. He would make his message appear to be gibberish to somebody but easily interpreted by you. Find the simplest formula possible, Jake. That's my suggestion."

"Hmm...that makes sense, Nick. I need something to fill my time. I'll play with it a little more before I give up. Thanks for your advice."

They offered each other a few more assurances before hanging up. Jake lay on the bed staring at the ceiling for a few minutes. A cobweb hung from the light fixture to the corner. He closed his eyes willing himself to sleep. Sleep didn't come. Dani and her team would focus on all the angles: organized crime, the mystery man, Dan Rivera, the baby's father, the Thorpes, the estate, and every other angle they uncovered. She insisted Jake pull back, and he agreed, considering Avery's issues. But he would not be able to sleep with numbers rolling around in his head again, especially after Nick's comments. He didn't need the band of numbers marching through his head again. Nick said the simpler the better. *What would it hurt to examine the numbers again?*

CHAPTER FORTY-ONE

JAKE THREW ON his robe and slippers and wandered to the office to sit at his desk. He ran his fingers through his hair as he examined the paper with the letters and numbers. He understood nothing about ciphers, other than what he learned from his recent research. If he accepted the premise that the "JS" at the front of the string meant Patterson knew he was in danger and wanted Jake to see the note, then the numbers must mean something. Nick suggested the formula would be simple enough for Jake to figure out but tough enough that whoever killed Patterson wouldn't understand it. The key would be to identify the simple formula. He decided to ignore the "JS" at the front with the assumption it meant Jake Scott. If nothing else, trying to solve the formula might exhaust him so he could fall asleep. Playing with the formula would also keep his mind off Avery lying in a hospital bed in Toronto.

He pulled a lined yellow pad of paper from a drawer and found a pen in the pile on the desk. Dani influenced the way the kitchen looked now, but she left Jake's office alone, for which he was grateful. Next, he logged onto the computer and typed "simple ciphers" into the search bar. The same results as his earlier research came up. The algorithms were not that simple. With mind bending names like Caesar cipher, Atbash cipher, Affine cipher, Baconian cipher, Rot13 cipher, it was enough to make his head explode. Jake decided he had to be missing something.

Realizing this could take a while, he got up to brew a pot of coffee in the kitchen. While the doctor told him he should reduce his coffee intake to eliminate digestive issues, he told himself this special occasion called for copious amounts of brew. His doctor would undoubtedly disagree, but at least it wasn't beer. He filled the carafe to the 12-cup mark and poured the water into the coffee maker's reservoir.

The sound of coffee dribbling into the carafe and the aroma of the brew filled the house as Jake wandered back to his office. He sat on his chair and typed a search that came to him when he prepared the coffee in the kitchen. *Code breaking numbers to letters.* The result looked more like what Nick referred to and what Jake now looked for. The search displayed a formula suggesting simply replacing the number "1" with "A," "2" with "B," etc. He wrote the number on the pad.

JS18421741919172019722009

Underneath, he wrote the alphabet and beneath that a corresponding number. His adrenalin rushed as he applied the formula to Patterson's message. The rush petered out when the result became a mess of letters meaning nothing.

He realized he needed to separate the numbers somehow. But how? For example, the first number could be letter number "1" or "18," so either "A" or "R." He checked his watch to see if it was too late to call Nick for advice. It was. Nick sounded like he desperately needed sleep during their last phone call, so Jake didn't bother him.

The coffee maker beeped, so he hurried to the kitchen to pour a cup, his mind on assorted permutations and combinations. Despite the setback with the first attempt, excitement raced through his veins. Sleep became a distant memory. He filled a cup and added his favorite vanilla creamer, something else the doctor told him to quit. The doctor seemed to want to cut everything good, but that was for another day. Jake returned to the office and continued to jot down various combinations, separating the numbers in different ways. No combination made sense.

A couple of hours later, Jake's head nodded despite the buzz from two additional cups of coffee he consumed. He sat back and stared blearily at the yellow pad resting on his knee. His robe hung askew; his hair shot out in every direction from the countless times he ran his fingers through it. The results of his experimentation so far—a page full of letters and numbers that meant nothing. No matter how he separated the numbers, nothing made sense. He had been at this for long enough. The numbers and letters blurred on the page, and his body sagged as if someone opened a valve and let the life drain out of him. A quick peek in the bedroom earlier revealed Oliver fast asleep on the end of the bed.

Jake tossed the pad of paper on the desk in frustration to join all the other documents and scribbled sheets of notes. He thought he was onto something, but if he was, he hadn't found the right formula. Two sheets fluttered to the floor from the stack. Too tired to pick them up, he decided they could lie on the floor until morning. He shuffled to the bedroom, shimmied out of his robe, tossed it on a chair, slipped out of his slippers, and flopped on the bed. He yanked the covers to his eyes.

But the numbers wouldn't leave him. Something Nick said collided with the numbers dancing in his brain. His tired mind tried to slow everything down to grasp the elusive thought. After a few minutes, his eyes popped open. This was becoming a habit, but he had an inkling. Nick said the cipher would be easy to solve but difficult enough that the answer wouldn't be obvious. Jake assumed the hard part was separating the numbers so the algorithm made sense, but what if it was more than that?

Jake recalled his search referred to other tricks for converting numbers to letters to encode a message. Things like using the alphabet backwards. For example, "Z" represented number "1."

He wondered how much coffee remained.

Newly energized, he threw off the covers again. Oliver opened one eye before going back to sleep. Jake pulled on his robe again, retrieved his mug from the office, and headed for the kitchen, thankful the carafe held enough coffee for a few more cups. The creamer container only offered a dribble, and he had neglected to buy more, so he made do with black coffee this time. The coffee buzz would be in overdrive after this, he thought.

He started with the premise that the last letter in the alphabet represented the number one. Once again, he tried different combinations of numbers. More and more gibberish. He took the last sip of coffee. His body buzzed now, not from any success but from the black coffee. He gave up on the formula and tried assigning "zero" to "A" instead of "one."

He tried splitting the numbers individually.

1 8 4 2 1 7 4 1 9 1 9 1 7 2 0 1 9 7 2 0 0 9 became BIECBHEB-JBJBHCABJHCAAJ. Once again, it meant nothing. He tried different combinations, starting with eighteen and then forty-two. He noticed earlier that some letters repeated, depending on how he arranged them, so he focused on that. He identified repeating number combinations and assigned letters to them using the new formula. He continued breaking the numbers into different combinations. He found two Es and three Ts and put them in their place with lines between them. It was like solving a puzzle on Wheel of Fortune. *May I buy a vowel, please?* Any notion of sleep disappeared as he scribbled letters, and the words coalesced.

Finally, he came up with the number combination 18 4 2 17 4 19 19 17 20 19 7 2 0 0 9. He sat back in his chair, staring in disbelief at the pad of paper. He was on his fourth sheet of scribblings and almost had it, but the last four letters stumped him. Had Petterson used a different formula or made a mistake in his haste when writing the message? Still, Jake was so close he could taste it.

The message read JSSECRETTRUTHCAAJ.

CHAPTER FORTY-TWO

JAKE PRIED HIS eyes open to bare skin against his face. He blinked several times as the overhead light still lit the room. As he regained consciousness and pushed himself upright, he realized he had fallen asleep on his arms, which leaned numbly on the desk. His empty cup sat at his left elbow on the verge of tumbling off the edge of the desk, and he had shoved some of the papers scattered on the desk onto the floor.

He sat up, shook his arms to wake them, and glanced at his watch. Seven a.m. A big stretch elicited a groan from a twinge in his back. He lifted his stiff body to a standing position, using the arms of the chair. He licked his dry lips, grimacing at the lingering aftertaste of last night's coffee. The thrumming in his head couldn't have felt worse if it was one of the hangovers he gave himself back in the day.

He checked his phone for a message from Nick, but there was nothing. He supposed that no news was good news, but he resolved to call his daughter's significant other within the hour if he hadn't heard from him.

The shower and his toothbrush beckoned. Breakfast could wait, and more coffee was out of the question for now. Oliver would demand his meal soon, but Jake picked up the yellow note pad from the desk and stared at it with equal parts satisfaction and frustration.

JSSECRETTRUTHCAAJ

JAKE SCOTT SECRET TRUTH CAAJ

What could it mean? Jake was sure if Patterson left the message for him and he deciphered it, all would become clear. But the message remained cryptic. Frustration outweighed satisfaction.

With a shoulder shrug, he tossed the pad back on the desk and wandered to the kitchen, where he found Oliver pawing at his dish, pushing it around the floor as if his food would magically appear with one more shove. The cat arched his back in appreciation as Jake petted him for about a minute until Oliver opted for food over a good scratch. Jake filled his dishes with food and water and headed to his bedroom.

With fresh clothes from the drawer, he moved into the bathroom. No sooner had he turned on the shower than his phone rang. Jake walked to the kitchen wearing only a white towel and sat, heaving a deep sigh of trepidation as he tapped the button to connect to the caller whose name appeared on the screen.

But it turned out Nick had nothing much to report. Avery had stayed in intensive care following the surgery, where the doctors monitored her progress and the baby's. He assured Jake that the doctors had told him it was normal procedure to stabilize the patient's condition. In short, Nick said, everybody had to cool their jets and wait for things to take their course. Jake and Nick agreed, there was nothing more difficult.

Jake told Nick about partially breaking the code. They discussed what CAAJ could mean, and neither came up with anything that made any sense. They agreed Patterson might have rushed at the end and made a mistake. Nick said his only suggestion was that Jake continue to try different combinations.

With an unnecessary promise from Nick that he would continue to keep Jake apprised, they disconnected. It went without saying Nick would call him the second anything happened, but Jake appreciated the reassurance.

When he returned to the bathroom, the hot running water steamed up the mirror so that he couldn't see his reflection. So eager was he to talk to Nick when the call came in, he forgot to turn off the tap. He climbed into the shower stall worrying about Avery, but he needed to push it from his mind, and the only way to do that was to concentrate on the damn numbers.

He pondered the letters CAAJ as he lathered himself. He wrote them on the steamed glass shower enclosure with his finger. Nothing jumped out as the bathroom light gleamed through the lettering as if calling to Jake. *I'm here. Figure me out.* He zeroed in on the two repeating letters. Had he combined the four numbers wrong? Mathematically, there were limited choices. *Why would Patterson go to the trouble of writing a code for him to find and decipher only to mess up the last four letters?* The possibility he rushed at the end seemed plausible.

Jake realized he could spend all day trying to figure out the mistake Patterson made if, in fact, that's what it was. Wait! Maybe Patterson hadn't made a mistake at all. Jake felt a glow of excitement again as he hurried to finish his shower and dry himself off.

He *had* to brush his teeth before rushing back to the office to test his theory. Even though he looked at the numbers for what seemed like a million times, he couldn't recall the last four digits clearly. He had focused on the letters. He thought he remembered but needed to refresh his memory by looking at them again. Out of necessity, it could wait a few more minutes until he banished the aftertaste of the coffee from his mouth with a good brushing and mouthwash.

Finally ready, he dressed in his favorite tan tee shirt with multicolored mountains emblazoned on the front and navy shorts and hurried back to the office, tossing his dirty clothes in the hamper on the way. The last four numbers were as he thought. He copied the numbers on a fresh piece of paper.

18 4 2 17 4 19 19 17 20 19 7 2 0 0 9

Underneath, he wrote the results of his work from the previous night.

JAKE SCOTT SECRET TRUTH CAAJ

And underneath that, he jotted the message he surmised Patterson intended for him.

JAKE SCOTT SECRET TRUTH 2009

Patterson wanted to tell him the year 2009 held the key to some secret truth.

CHAPTER FORTY-THREE

JAKE COULDN'T CONTAIN his excitement. It had to be right. Something happened in 2009, fifteen years ago, that would help explain the explosion. But doubts crept in. He could be totally off base, fooling himself into believing he had cracked the message. He needed to talk to Dani to bring her up to speed on Avery and to discuss his findings with her.

She answered his call right away. Jake explained that Avery had remained stable and all they could do was wait. Then he veered to the message. Since she told him to leave it alone, he knew to tread carefully.

"By the way, I was sitting around the house feeling sorry for myself last night, so I took another crack at the message Patterson left behind."

Silence, which Jake took as his signal to continue.

"Nick reminded me that if Patterson left the message for me, the decoding algorithm would be simple yet complicated enough that anyone else seeing it may not comprehend the meaning or have the time to decipher it. I tried various algorithms to see what I could come up with."

"Um-hm," was Dani's response.

Jake said, "To make a long story short, I'm sure now he did intend the message for me, and I cracked it."

Dani perked up. "Okay," she said, "let's set aside for the moment that you ignored me when I asked you to leave it alone. I admit, I'm curious, Jake Scott. What did you find out?"

Jake said, "Let's say you were right about the first two letters, which means he intended the message for me." He told her about his initial findings related to the first part of the number sequence and how the last four numbers, 2009, translated to CAAJ, which made no sense. "Since the last four numbers don't translate to anything, it's possible they weren't intended to be translated. He might've been trying to tell me about a secret truth from 2009 he wanted me, uh, us, to investigate." Jake's voice rose to match his excitement level. "I think the message reads, 'Jake Scott, secret truth 2009.'"

Dani stayed silent for a full minute. Finally, she said, "Okay, I won't suggest you're wrong, Jake. I have nothing better to propose regarding the string of numbers. I'm sure you worked for hours on this. The problem is that the unscrambled message sends the investigation in a totally different direction. If you're correct, we should focus our attention on 2009. But it's so flimsy. My constables are investigating the different motives we discussed. It's like they're chasing phantoms. They haven't proved or disproved any of them. You might have discovered something here, Jake, but it's tenuous at best. Other options we discussed the other night seemed more solid. Tell me something and don't take this wrong. You didn't force your formula to fit some preconceived notion of what Patterson tried to do, did you?"

"No, of course not, Dani. My findings resulted from trial and error and countless cups of coffee. I agree it's weak, but I'm convinced enough to follow up; do a little research on things that happened in 2009. Try to find something concrete enough for you and your team to follow up."

"I don't know, Jake. If Patterson tried to send you a message and ended up dead because of it, you could be in danger, especially if organized crime is involved. Did the dark car show up again?"

"No, but I don't even need to leave the house to research this. I'll do everything on my computer. It will take a load off everything you're doing. And I promise I'll keep you posted every step of the way. It will help me keep my mind off Avery, too."

"Well, since you'll do it no matter what I say, see what you can find out. If there's something to it, I'll reassign a constable. But if the dark car shows up again, call me immediately. I'll send someone over."

"That's fair, Dani. You have my word. I've learned from previous adventures not to get too involved."

Dani chuckled ruefully. "Yeah, well, I don't believe *that* for a second. Be careful, Jake, whatever you do. I hope you find something useful so we can finish this. Please give my regards to Nick and Avery and remind Nick that I'm happy to talk to Avery anytime she's ready."

"I certainly will, dear. Hope to see you soon. Hugs!"

CHAPTER FORTY-FOUR

JAKE GOT OFF the phone and searched the local news headlines online for 2009. Like all searches, this one produced more results than he could handle. Over 1.3 million, to be precise. Even though he asked specifically for Ottawa, the result at the top of the page read, *Most-read Canadian news stories of 2009.* The headline referred to two high-profile murders in Ontario, neither of which took place in Ottawa. Nothing in Patterson's message pointed to the city, province, or even the country, for that matter, so Jake bookmarked the news items in case he wanted to circle back to do more research. He discovered that President Obama had visited Ottawa that year, which accounted for the headlines that had been shown in response to his search. The nationwide highlights for 2009 included the recession, the Swine Flu, a Newfoundland helicopter crash, and the car industry collapse. Jake recalled them all, but none fit the criteria he was looking for.

He searched for "the Biggest stories in Ottawa in 2009." That produced a handful of results. A tornado ripped through the region in April, and police charged a man for a murder in the city on New Year's Day. The felony caseload increased by 21% in 2009 from the previous year, gang violence declined... Interesting reading, but nothing so far that triggered further investigation. Surely, Patterson's message pointed to something more obvious.

Jake searched for missing persons. The site referred readers to a social media page for albums holding photos of those who had disappeared, some of which dated back much further than 2009. A fourteen-year-old boy went missing in 2009, and no one had heard from him since. According to the article, many readers offered tips, and police spoke to hundreds of people, but the case remained unsolved. Jake pondered the case. If that was what Patterson referred to, he had no idea what steps he would take to follow up. He guessed he would start with the boy's parents. With Patterson dead, he didn't know whom else he could talk to. He felt sorry for the family, bookmarked the page, and moved on.

Jake leaned back in his chair with his hands behind his head, staring at the screen and ruminating over his findings. He tried to put himself in Patterson's shoes. Patterson must have assumed he was in danger. He must have known about some secret that happened in 2009, which he had planned to divulge to Jake that night. So worried he wouldn't have time to talk to Jake that he took a few minutes to prepare an encrypted message he tucked in his pocket. *What could it be?* Something happened in 2009 that no one knew about except Patterson and, obviously, someone else who wanted to silence him. Did it have something to do with organized crime? Selling fake rugs? Something else?

Jake leaned forward again and threw everything that came to mind at the browser's search bar, coming up with a variety of topics. He bookmarked a few he thought he would go back to if nothing more promising surfaced, but his searches revealed little. He still held onto the hope he would know it when he saw it.

After continual searches with no result, he rested his elbow on the arm of the chair with his face in his palm while tapping words with one finger on his other hand into the search engine and scrolling with the mouse. Another search produced a list of uninteresting headlines, but one caught his attention. Unsolved murders. He scrolled to the page and found two in Ottawa in 2009. One, a twenty-six-year-old man named Harold Gratton whom police linked to a gang. Someone gunned him down in May 2009 inside a crowded bar in the Byward Market. No witnesses came forward, and no murder weapon was ever found. Since police linked him to a gang, there could be an international organized crime element, so the story stood out as a possibility.

The grainy photo with the article had been photoshopped to remove someone. Gratton had an oval face with eyebrows that sloped downward in the middle. He wore a trimmed beard and wavy hair combed to the left. He looked like any twenty-something-year-old with his entire life in front of him. Jake wondered how he could have become mixed up with a gang. The lure of easy money or drug dependency usually dragged them in.

The second article referred to a female university student whose battered body was found in the river in September 2009. Cause of death was determined to be drowning, but because of the bruising, police suspected foul play. Like the young man gunned down in the Market, no witnesses came forward. Jake remembered the cases from his days at the paper, but the editor hadn't assigned them to him. He searched the internet for online articles covering the story and found a piece written by his friend and former colleague, Janice Richardson.

Jake had a passing interest at the time and probably read Janice's article to offer suggestions before she submitted it to the editor, but since he had no direct involvement, he couldn't recall much about the story. Janice was a new hire, and according to her column, police couldn't account for the young woman's whereabouts from about ten o'clock at night until around seven o'clock the next morning when someone walking their dog discovered her body. Police interviewed her family and university friends but, according to the paper, didn't identify anyone of interest.

The picture accompanying the column showed a vibrant, smiling young woman. It appeared the woman had taken a selfie at a beach. The photo was slightly off-kilter, with the horizon tilting to the right. The top of the woman's head to mid-chest were visible, and the black-and-white photo revealed a light-colored bathing suit with shoulder straps. Wind swept her shoulder-length hair to one side. Her broad smile raised her cheeks into apple shapes underneath the dark irises of her eyes. She had a broad nose but not too much. Her features combined to make her into a pretty young woman. She appeared to be happy and enjoying her time in the sun. Gone too soon. Her name was Cynthia Harmer.

The familiar juices flowed through Jake. Something prickled at the back of his neck, the same sensation he got as an investigative reporter when he closed in on an exclusive. Patterson's message could have pointed to either of these cases. The articles gave him a place to start. None of the other instances he bookmarked called to him like these two did. The organized crime angle suggested Patterson's message pointed to Harold Gratton, the man gunned down in the Market. Logical given Patterson's violent death. But Jake's intuition told him it had something to do with Cynthia Harmer. His intuition steered him wrong before, but more times than not, it pushed him in the right direction.

He dialed Janice Richardson.

CHAPTER FORTY-FIVE

"JAKE SCOTT," JANICE Richardson exclaimed. "I assumed you must be living in a beach house in the Caribbean somewhere since you never call, but here you are calling me to invite me for lunch."

Janice hadn't changed. Jake mentored her early in her career, and she became an excellent reporter in her own right. Eventually, she found the confidence to trade barbs with her former mentor, and they became close friends. They had gone for lunch to reminisce three weeks earlier, but every time Jake called, she would imply they hadn't seen each other in years. Jake settled into the role of father figure to Janice, and she often picked his brain. She climbed the ranks at the newspaper, and Jake couldn't be prouder.

They exchanged pleasantries for a few minutes, catching up on the city's recent events. Jake agreed it was his turn to buy lunch, and with a promise to arrange a date soon, he turned to the subject he wanted to talk about.

"Do you remember two murders from 2009? You wrote articles about each of them when you were a newcomer to the paper. You showed them to me before you submitted them to the editor. A young man named Harold Gratton was shot in the Market, and a young university student named, uh just a second, oh, yes, Cynthia Harmer was found in the river. Neither have been solved."

"Oh, boy. What are you into now, Jake Scott? Trying to do the police's job again?" Janice chuckled. "From what you told me last time, Dani Perez might be a little ticked off if you're involved in something you shouldn't be. You can remove the boy from the investigation, but you can't remove the investigation from the boy, right? Yes, I remember the articles. Talk about baptism by fire. I couldn't believe the boss assigned the stories to me, but I remember you were busy on another story. You helped me through it, though. I've been musing about writing another piece on unsolved murders in Ottawa. There are too many. I expect readers to be interested in knowing that the police don't just give up. Why are you interested in these two?"

Jake gave her the highlights of the explosion at the Bed and Breakfast and how he had been trying to help Dani with the case with her approval. He told her about the cryptic note Patterson left and how he came up with the two names.

"Wow, that's impressive investigative work. You're the best, Jake. Really! I would love to write about this."

"Maybe later, Janice, if anything comes of the investigation. I'll mention it to Dani. I could be chasing my tail, but anything you can tell me would be helpful."

"Well, I have to dig out my notes, but as I recall, the Gratton case seemed like a professional hit. Give me a second."

Jake discerned the tapping of computer keys.

"Got it," Janice said. "The shooter walked up to Gratton in front of a pile of people in broad daylight, shot him, hopped on a motorcycle, and sped off. Most of the people in the area didn't even see him, and the ones who did said he wore a motorcycle helmet with a dark face shield. They were going about their business and didn't look until they heard the pop of the gun. It's the same principle as a red light/green light accident. No one pays attention until they hear the crash. Then they watch the cars spinning around while they reach for their phones to get a video for social media. Nobody knows who's at fault except the drivers; both will say it wasn't them.

"Even the ones who say they spotted the shooter said he had a slight build that made his helmeted head seem oversized for his body. He wore jeans and a leather jacket. They all agreed the shooter was male, though, for what that's worth. Everybody was in shock, so nobody caught the bike's license number. The police later found the bike tucked beside a dumpster behind a Canadian Tire store on Bank Street. Somebody must've picked the shooter up, and they took the back roads back to the rock they emerged from under."

Jake took notes and chuckled at Janice's reference to no one describing the shooter. Her observation reminded him of Dani's Shrek versus Brad Pitt comment. He reflected on the Demirs and their association with organized crime. Whoever blew up the Bed and Breakfast might have had ties to the fake rug money laundering scheme. Maybe the mystery man Gladis Knight saw leaving the Bed and Breakfast was also the shooter from 2009. Maybe that's what Patterson wanted to tell him. Too many "maybes." He noted the Demirs, Patterson, and Harold Gratton on his yellow pad and drew heavy lines between them. He traced the lines back and forth on the paper until his pen almost wore through the page when Janice interrupted him.

"Jake, are you still with me?"

He realized he had been silent while he mulled over Janice's recounting of the shooting. He heard more tapping.

"Yes, I'm sorry, Janice. I'm still here. Sorry, I got distracted rationalizing connections to the Bed and Breakfast."

"Okay, I found my notes on Cynthia Harmer. My notes aren't that good. I owe you an enormous debt of gratitude for forcing me to keep proper folders on the computer for my notes, but I recall it was after this. Maybe *I* should buy *you* lunch."

"This one stuck with me for a while," she said. "There seemed to be a cone of silence over the case. Cynthia lived off campus in an apartment. A friend said she went home after class as usual, and no one saw her again until a dog walker found her the next morning. Yet, others said she went to a party and disappeared. They speculated she might have gone off with some guy, but nobody saw her leave. At least, they say they didn't. I tried to track down anybody who would say something, but it was like nobody wanted to talk. Apparently, the police didn't get anywhere with them either. Some friends! I remember her professors saying she worked hard, did well in school. She was athletic but a bit of a loner. Nobody would even speculate about what might have happened. Nobody would point fingers, although I sensed several seemed to know something. I dug and dug and came up empty."

Jake wrote furiously as Janice spoke. "Did you record the names of people you talked to, Janice? I have time to follow up."

"Not all, but I can do one better. I can send a picture of a person I talked to. Cynthia had a page on social media with pictures of friends, and I took a screenshot of the one I interviewed. Someone took the site down shortly after that. That's difficult to do, but somehow the family or their lawyers made it happen, I guess. Just a sec. I'll forward the pic to you. I don't see his name here, but it's in my notes."

Jake waited a few seconds until his phone pinged. He opened the email from Janice with no subject header and clicked on the attachment. His heart skipped a beat as the picture appeared on the screen. The photo showed a shirtless, tanned man standing on a pier with a huge grin splitting his face. He stood in front of a fishing boat, holding a beer in one hand, and a large trout dangling at the end of a pole in the other. It seemed to Jake like he froze in time as he stared at the picture. Despite the floppy hat shading the man's face, he was still identifiable to Jake.

"You don't need to find the man's name, Janice. I know who he is." The man holding the pole and fish was none other than Craig Thorpe.

CHAPTER FORTY-SIX

"VERY INTERESTING," WAS Dani's response when Jake told her about his discussion with Janice Richardson. "It's even more interesting because we pulled Craig's medical files. Doctors diagnosed his PTSD as severe enough that he had uncontrollable thoughts about whatever event caused his illness. The doctor wouldn't discuss Craig's case specifically, but he said in cases like his, something could trigger a memory that would put him right back into the event. I queried the doctor in general terms about someone with that condition believing they had to destroy an enemy or save everyone by turning the gas on. He agreed it could be possible. I don't know what the connection would be to Cynthia Harmer, but you've given us another angle to investigate."

As he spoke with Dani, Jake sat in his recliner with his feet up in the sunroom, watching a black squirrel bounce along the top of the fence at the back of the yard. "It's scary to think that PTSD could be uncontrollable like that. Thorpe's mother said nothing about the seriousness of his PTSD. I suppose that puts Craig at the top of the suspect list. Did the medical records show when the incident took place that caused Craig's PTSD?"

"Recently. I believe 2022. I'm intrigued by both murders in 2009.

Our Guns and Gangs Unit would have investigated the first one you mentioned, Harold Gratton. I'll follow up with them too for more information about the gang Gratton was involved with. I'll connect them to the Fraud guys who are looking into the money laundering angle with the Demirs's Turkish rug operation for any kind of link."

The squirrel reached the end of the fence and leaped out of sight to a tree in the neighbor's yard.

"And the Cynthia Harmer murder?" Jake asked.

"I wasn't in the department when they investigated that one, Jake. I was working in Sudbury at the time. Let me check the file on her murder. Just a second. Oh, here it is. Ah, of course! My old boss, Enzo Leblanc, led the investigation."

"Leblanc? I remember him. He's the one that kind of rushed to judgment to clear a case just before he retired. Didn't he die a few months ago?"

"That's the one, and yes, he did. His knowledge about the case is gone. Record keeping wasn't his strong suit. I'll dig out what's on file. Hopefully, one of the investigators kept good notes. Oh, we're going to make an arrest in the Byward Market stabbing in the next twenty-four hours. It's going to be nice to put that one to bed. We're completing the paperwork to make sure the charges stick."

"Congratulations, Dani! That's awesome. I'm so happy for you."

Dani thanked Jake again for the information he dug up. They chatted for a few more minutes before disconnecting.

Jake sat in his chair, musing about the surprises the explosion uncovered. He couldn't get over the fact every person staying at the Bed and Breakfast kept secrets.

THE SECRET TRUTH.

That's what Patterson's message said.

Jake didn't believe for a second that he had uncovered a secret truth yet. Craig Thorpe knew the victim, Cynthia Harmer, but there had to be more. Surprising, that's all. It didn't reveal any startling explanation for the explosion. Perhaps Craig set off the explosion because of a flashback to a previous incident, but there had to be more.

What could it be?

Jake climbed out of his chair to return to his office. He nearly stepped on Oliver, who was lying in the hallway. The cat rolled onto his back for a rub, which Jake obliged. He reached his office and lifted the top of his laptop to wake it up. The computer opened to the page about Cynthia's murder. He reread the article to find out which program she enrolled in at the university.

The clock above his printer read 4:48 p.m. He wondered if anyone would be available to talk to at the university. Another five minutes of searching turned up a phone number for the science faculty. He dialed and waited to see if anyone remained in the office. A woman answered.

Jake explained the reason for his call: that he was a former reporter looking for information on a cold case involving Cynthia Harmer. He embellished the story by saying he planned to write a book about unsolved murders in the area and that the call was part of his research. He told her that Cynthia studied in the Commerce program.

The woman asked, "Do you know if she studied accounting? Finance? International Business? Entrepreneurship? They're all part of the Commerce program. That's only some of them."

"I'm sorry, I don't know any of that. I hoped you could look her up on your computer and point me in the right direction."

The woman heaved a heavy sigh like he asked her to abandon everything she was doing and work until midnight. She said, "You said 2009, right? I started working here in 2010. Let me see what I can find." Soft music played on the phone while Jake waited. A few moments later, she came back on the line.

"I found her in the system. She studied accounting. I know someone who's been the head of that department for years. You say someone murdered the poor girl? That's horrible. Let me see if Professor Carpenter is still in his office."

Jake thanked her and waited. While he did, he thought about Fletcher Patterson being an accountant and Cynthia Harmer in the accounting program. Another strange coincidence.

To Jake's surprise, Professor Carpenter answered, but his voice sounded rushed.

"How can I help you? You're calling kind of late. Please make this quick. I'm scheduled for an appointment and was about to leave. If you're calling about your son or daughter, tell me what you need, and I'll get back to you tomorrow."

Jake settled into his chair, anticipating this would be a colossal waste of his time based on the man's attitude. That his call would go nowhere. He said, "I'm not calling about my son or daughter, Professor. I'm interested in learning more about a young woman named Cynthia Harmer, who studied in your program. Someone murdered her in 2009. That was fifteen years ago, but I'm hoping you can offer some information." Jake detected an intake of breath when he mentioned Cynthia's name. He reiterated his white lie about researching a book. Carpenter listened without uttering a word. Then the professor said something that perked Jake up enough to lean forward in his chair.

"I would like very much to talk about that. Please bear with me while I close my door."

CHAPTER FORTY-SEVEN

"IT'S BEEN A long time since someone mentioned her name," Carpenter said. "What's your interest in the case again? You're writing a book?"

Jake sensed the professor would be forthcoming, so he leveled with the man. "I'm not being completely honest with you. I was nearly killed in the recent explosion in Westboro. It turns out Cynthia knew one of the victims in the explosion, so I'm following up, trying to piece things together. A friend works in Homicide at the Ottawa Police Service, and I'm doing some preliminary investigation to help her. I'm a former investigative reporter, now retired." Jake left out the part about the cryptic message he received from Patterson.

"Well, I wasn't being totally honest with you, either sir. I have no appointment scheduled. I find it difficult to get out of here on time often, so when I get a late phone call, I use the appointment excuse. Yes, I recall Cynthia was a very bright student. One of the best students I ever had, in fact. I like to take a particular interest in students who are above average." The professor added hastily, "That's not to say I don't pay attention to all my students. But if someone is exceedingly bright, I try to guide them along the best study path to maximize their career opportunities. It saddened me when I learned about her death. Quite a shock! I even attended her funeral."

Jake could relate to this, as he did the same by attending Patterson's funeral, albeit for a different reason.

The professor continued. "I read nothing but the financial section and occasionally the obituaries these days. When you get to my age, the financial news and the obituaries can be depressing enough. I overheard students talking about the explosion. The news is too depressing and usually too slanted. Oh, sorry, you said you were a former reporter. No offense."

Jake chuckled. "None taken, Professor. I agree with you. I'm happy I'm not working in the media now. But back to the reason for my call, do you know anything about a relationship between Craig Thorpe and Cynthia Harmer?"

"Craig Thorpe. That name doesn't ring any bells. Let me check to see if he went to this school. I don't think he attended any of my classes."

Jake doubted that the man could remember the names of every person who had attended his classes over the years. But when Carpenter came back on the line, he confirmed the information. "No, no one by that name was in my class. I checked my attendee stats. I'm pretty good with names, though."

Jake said, "Okay, Thorpe is in the military, so he probably went to a military school."

"Yes, yes," the professor said.

Jake wondered if he had stumbled upon the stereotypical absent-minded professor.

Professor Carpenter then said, "I did my own investigating, you know, when young Cynthia died. The police weren't getting anywhere, so I followed up myself. I told the authorities everything I found out. I talked to friends of Cynthia's and friends of friends. They opened up to me when they wouldn't to the police. You know how young people are. Sometimes, they don't trust authority. But they trusted me because I worked to gain their confidence. I try to get to know my class attendees so I can apply the best possible teaching methods to inspire them. Some told me Cynthia attended a party at a park with friends that night. It was the beginning of the school year. They said she got drunk to the point of being nonresponsive. She apparently woke up, slipped away, and went for a swim. They couldn't account for her bruises. They all said they didn't know what happened to her. But someone knows."

"Why do you say that, Professor?"

"By the way they talked. Like they made an agreement to keep things quiet. Something happened that night that everyone kept hush-hush. I identified everyone who attended the party. I talked to them collectively and individually, but I couldn't crack their code of silence. The police couldn't either. Even to this day, some, if not all, the young people at the party that night know more than they're letting on."

Jake said, "Would you mind looking at the newspaper article about the explosion? It includes photos of the deceased. You said you don't know Craig Thorpe, but maybe you would recognize him if you saw him."

"I can do that. What was the date again?"

Jake told him the date and pulled the page up on his own computer. He waited until the professor came back on the line. When he did, he sent a shockwave through Jake that left him shaking.

CHAPTER FORTY-EIGHT

"I DON'T RECOGNIZE THE man identified as Craig Thorpe, but I recognize several of the others even though they're a few years older in the picture. They were at the party. Every one of them. The first two are Omar Demir and Seda Aydin. They dated, as I recall, so it looks like they married. Her married name would be Demir. I remember the woman identified as Francis Thorpe as Brenda Rutledge. I wonder why her name is different. That's definitely her. They all hung around together with Cynthia Harmer. I didn't recognize the woman identified in the article as Willow Altman. I talked to Omar, Seda, and Brenda after the party. They must have had a reunion at the Bed and Breakfast or something. It's strange I didn't see any of their names in the obituaries. I guess I didn't read the obituaries the day they were published in the paper. Like I said, I don't read them every day."

Jake had difficulty finding his voice as he considered the enormity of Carpenter's words. *Was the professor a crackpot, or did nearly every one of the people staying at the Bed and Breakfast attend university together?* As Jake thought back, he remembered telling Dani they were all around the same age. Except Willow. She was younger.

The question of why anyone would blow up a houseful of people had always nagged at him. Unless the person was insane, like Thorpe may have been, or just didn't care, like organized crime. *But did this case circle back to something to do with Cynthia's death?*

"Are you there, sir?"

"Yes, I'm here," Jake answered. "It's a shock to hear you say they all knew each other. You stumped me with Brenda Rutledge, but then I remembered she changed her name somewhere along the way."

"Why would she do that?"

"She was convicted of pretending to be a nurse and giving someone the wrong prescription, so after a bit of jail time, she changed her name to start over. It was around that time she met Craig Thorpe."

Carpenter said, "The twists and turns of life are strange sometimes, aren't they? These kids had their whole lives ahead of them. I don't know what happened at the party, but I think they made a serious error in judgment in 2009, and it came back to haunt them. I'm not sure how, but it seems if they did something bad at the party, karma took over with that horrible explosion. To think they would all be in the same house when it exploded. What a coincidence!"

Jake didn't believe it was a coincidence at all, but he let the professor think what he wanted. He decided he really admired the professor for the way he tackled his teaching assignment and cared for his students. He said, "I appreciate your honesty, and I'm sorry I've kept you beyond your normal departure time. I'd like to buy you a coffee sometime as a thank you." Jake wanted to ask Carpenter about Fletcher Patterson when the professor responded.

"I would like that, Mr. Scott. The coffee, I mean. Before you go, though, there's one thing I forgot to mention. Two other people attended the party who seemed to have escaped the explosion. One was a fellow who attended my class. He was also an excellent student and I believe he went on to have a career as an accountant. His name is Fletcher Patterson."

"Yes, I know of Fletcher Patterson. I met him at the Bed and Breakfast, but he got lucky and left before the explosion. Who was the other person?"

"The other person didn't attend university, but I knew about him through the grapevine. I don't recall his name, and I never met him, but he was Cynthia's older brother."

Jake had a lot to ponder when he disconnected, but his first thought was for Avery. He called Nick, who picked up the call right away. Nick had seen Avery for a short time in intensive care and reported that she seemed exhausted but in good spirits. The doctors told him they would move her into a regular bed over the next day or so if she continued to progress at her current rate.

It relieved Jake to hear the news, but because Avery needed her rest, he declined to speak to her. He asked Nick to let her know he promised he would talk to her soon.

Jake's next call was to Dani. Her breathing sounded labored as she answered the phone. He heard hurried footsteps.

"Sorry, Jake. I'm on my way to a murder scene. A passerby found a body in a car at Mooney's Bay Park. Can you imagine? People are around that park all the time. Anyway, what's up?"

"I learned something interesting, Dani. It turns out the Demirs, Francis Thorpe, AKA Brenda Rutledge, and Fletcher Patterson all attended university together with Cynthia Harmer. I spoke with a Professor Carpenter at the university, and he told me this. They all knew each other! He said they went to a party together the night Cynthia died. He's convinced something went terribly wrong at the party, and they all know what happened. He also said Cynthia had an older brother who went to the party."

A ding signifying the arrival of an elevator echoed through the phone.

The elevator dinged again. Dani said, "Listen, I'll call you back. Sorry. Let's talk about this either later tonight or tomorrow. If you don't hear from me, don't wait up. We'll talk tomorrow."

Jake heard Dani opening a car door.

"Okay, be safe, Dani."

Jake's mind swirled when he disconnected the call. Despite Nick's assurances, his concern for Avery and the baby were top of mind. He had been so happy, although a little taken aback, when Avery announced her pregnancy. Everything took a back seat to Avery's accident and subsequent surgery. He couldn't wait to talk to her again; to give her a big hug.

The professor's revelation about the connection between most of the people at the B&B satisfied Jake. Dani would direct her team to talk to Professor Carpenter and search for the brother the next day. He was confident her team would uncover the truth that had been secret for fifteen years. A little sleuthing and a lot of dumb luck brought him to this point. Now, he planned to focus on Avery's condition, which far outweighed any excitement about having come this far with the case.

Jake prepared a meal of scrambled eggs and toast for supper. He dragged his exhausted body through the routine of cooking. He glanced outside as he carried his plate down the hall and settled into his recliner. Long shadows darkened the grass along the fence in the backyard as dusk descended on the neighborhood. The flowers near the water trickling down the rocks into a small pond in the back corner rocked in the breeze.

A quick glance at his watch confirmed the time had flown since he spoke to the professor. An early bedtime beckoned him. He reminded himself to make a note to call the professor back in a day or two to invite him for the coffee he promised.

When he finished his meal, he rose from his chair with a grunt and absent-mindedly scraped the remnants into the recyclable bin in the kitchen and rinsed the dishes in the sink before placing them in the dishwasher. His phone rang in the sunroom. Could be Nick, he thought. He hurried to the sunroom to answer. To his surprise, it was Dani again. Jake let Oliver into the backyard to do his business, carried the phone into his bedroom, and sat on the bed. He hoped Dani had an early night and that she would drop over, but it was just the opposite.

"Jake, I'm at the crime scene of the murder at Mooney's Bay, and I took a couple of pictures. I'd like you to see them. I'm sending them right now. I'll stay on the phone until you've seen them."

"Okay, but wh..?"

"I've sent them. Let me know when you get them."

Jake's phone pinged, announcing the arrival of the photos. He worried about pressing the wrong key and cutting Dani off when he opened the pictures, but the little red box in the upper left corner of the phone still counted off the seconds, suggesting she was still there. When he clicked on the photos, his body stiffened. This night was full of surprises. The pictures showed the head and shoulders of a dead man and a car.

And he recognized both.

CHAPTER FORTY-NINE

THE MAN IN the first photograph stared wide-eyed back at Jake as if shocked by something. His shaggy brown hair hung over his ears, and he wore a gray jacket with a white logo on the sleeve. Jake recognized the man as the one he saw standing at the door of the hotel and again in the restaurant. The same man who drove slowly by the house. It was the man Jake thought was watching him. The other photo revealed a dark blue Chrysler 300 car, the same color and shape as the one he thought he saw frequently, most recently at Fletcher Patterson's funeral.

*

As Jake tried to pull himself together, a large shadowy figure hurried down the street toward his house. He wore unusually dark clothing considering the humid weather, and even more unusual was the hood pulled over his head and black leather gloves. He turned his face away from the street toward the cedar shrubs on Jake's neighbor's property. He checked the house number and turned in at Jake's laneway. When he reached the wooden gate, he reached over the top to unlatch the lock. The man stopped in the shadows of the corner of Jake's house, where he removed his running shoes. He stood listening but only detected the hum of crickets calling to each other.

*

Jake heard muffled footsteps and unintelligible talking in hushed tones in the background at the crime scene Dani was investigating. He imagined the various people scurrying about doing their jobs. Police officers would have cordoned off the scene, and the coroner would examine the body and make a preliminary estimate of time of death. Crime scene technicians would take pictures and document physical evidence. Dani would interview witnesses.

Jake said, "I can confirm this is the man I saw twice at the hotel, and he looks like the one who drove by my house. The car could be the one I kept seeing. Not that I feel any better, but at least the photos might confirm what I saw. Is the logo on his jacket the name of an electrical company?"

Dani confirmed it was. "And I'll bet my next pay cheque he was in the house the day of the explosion. I think Gladis was right all along. I suspect he did something with the wiring for the new electric stove installed at the B&B. He might have even altered the light switch in the basement to ensure the spark would set off the explosion."

*

The shadowy figure in Jake's yard didn't notice the dirt he stepped in on the top of the concrete steps as he tried sliding the patio door. To his surprise, the door moved easily, and it was unlocked. It had to be his lucky night. He nudged the door soundlessly to the side enough so that he could squeeze through.

*

"Is the deceased Cynthia Harmer's brother?" Jake asked.

Dani said, "Not unless he changed his name. His driver's license identifies him as Warren Belton."

"How did he die?"

"Strangulation with a rope wrapped around his neck. It's not the same method the killer used on Patterson. No knife involved this time. It looks like the killer sat in the back seat, wrapped the rope around Belton's neck, and used the backseat for leverage. The lack of defense wounds suggests Belton knew his killer. He didn't seem to put up a lot of resistance until he had the rope around his neck. Just like at the Patterson scene, there are no preliminary fingerprints to help us identify the killer."

*

The shadowy figure left a large, dirty footprint on the kitchen floor as he stepped inside the house and slid the door closed again. Oliver arrived at the door just as it closed and stared up at the man, waiting to be let in. The man turned away and stopped with one foot poised in front of the other, his ears tuned to Jake's conversation in the bedroom.

*

Jake recalled the cigarette burns on Fletcher Patterson. "I remember the guy at the door of the hotel smoking. If Patterson didn't have any cigarettes, this guy would. It sounds like you think he may be the person who set off the explosion at the B&B."

Dani replied, "The electrical company logo makes it quite possible. He would have an excuse to be in the house. He could have turned the valve on the gas line, but why? What's his motive? And why did someone want him dead? If there's a connection between the Patterson murder and this one, I'm really concerned for your safety. Someone may have killed Patterson because he knew too much. It could be the same motive for poor Belton here. You might be in danger if the killer knows you're digging into the case. I'm going to reassign the officer who's been cruising past your house to park in the front. At least for tonight."

*

The big man took quick, stealthy steps through the kitchen and down the hall to the closet, where he pushed aside the coats to make room. The hangers screeched on the rod holding the coats. He climbed in and slid the door closed again.

*

Jake detected a noise but remembered Oliver was still outside and probably scratched at the door to be let in. He called out, "Just a minute, Oliver. I'll be right there." To Dani, he said, "Do you really think that's necessary? I'm exhausted, so I'm going to bed early tonight. I'll put on the alarm and lock the doors. It'll be like Fort Knox here."

"I don't know what to think, Jake. I'm wondering about the brother that's running around out there somewhere. He could be behind all of this."

"Okay, if you assign an officer, please tell him not to come to the door. I plan on being sound asleep by the time he gets here."

*

The man in the closet had trouble hearing the conversation with the doors closed. He waited.

*

"Okay, Jake, fair enough. I must talk to a few people to determine if they saw anything. Lots of onlookers standing around, but I'm not sure how helpful they'll be. Put on your alarm now, and I'll call you in the morning. Oh, before I go, any word about Avery?"

"Still the same, Dani. Still in intensive care and being monitored. Hopefully, good news tomorrow."

They hung up, and Jake wandered down the hall to the front of the house. The security alarm Dani and Avery both insisted he install after the last trouble he got into could wait until he let Oliver back inside the house. As he passed the hall closet, a weird, sudden, icy sensation came over him. An unexplainable shiver. It had to be the idea of someone coming to harm him Dani put in his head. Jake satisfied himself the lock on the front door was secure.

Jake filled a glass with water from the tap, still strangely unsettled, almost insecure. He shut off the light and pushed the curtains back on the window but saw no sign of the police officer yet or a dark car. No doubt the officer would show up soon. Jake felt too exhausted to wait up for the policeman to arrive, but he had to admit he would sleep better knowing the officer sat outside.

Jake set the glass in the sink and sauntered down the hall to the sunroom. The involuntary shudder hit him again on the way past the closet. Despite his exhaustion and the officer who would be parked outside, he wondered if he would sleep thanks to the bogeyman Dani planted in his brain. When Jake arrived at the patio door, a dirty footprint on the floor startled him. His mind whirled as he tried to remember how or when he put the smudge there. *It had to be him. Who else could it have been?* He didn't realize a man had emerged from the closet behind him.

Oliver sat on the concrete step on the other side of the glass door, staring at him and meowing incessantly. His brown face, with its black stripes and large yellow eyes, looked startled. His ears stood straight up.

At the last second, Jake perceived a footfall behind him. The large man closed in on him with the speed and stealth of a jungle cat. A sudden jolt of pain and a shroud of dark nothingness overcame Jake. Oliver jumped back from the step as Jake crashed to the floor.

CHAPTER FIFTY

A DISTANT VOICE CALLED his name. The person sounded like a towel covered his mouth, but the voice became louder and clearer the longer Jake listened. His head throbbed like somebody drummed on it. As he pried his eyes open, brightness filtered in from the overhead light, causing his head to pulsate even more. He glimpsed the hardwood floor beyond his knees.

He tried to lift his hand to rub his eyes, but it wouldn't move. Trying to lift both hands accomplished nothing. A letter opener wouldn't slide between his wrists and the arms of the chair to which he seemed to be glued. His mind refused to accept what was happening as his eyes flew open. *Am I paralyzed?* He tried to stand to prove to himself he could move, but his feet wouldn't budge either. His legs were bent at the knee but immobile. He fought against the restrictions, but no matter how hard he tried, he couldn't move. His fingers and toes worked when he wiggled them. *Thank God, they moved.* He tried to recall what happened. He blacked out when he was about to let Oliver in, but why?

Movement to his right caught his attention, and he swiveled his head in that direction. Too fast! The motion sent stars shooting through his brain and elicited an involuntary groan. The sight shocked him. A large man sat to his right in a chair that Jake indignantly and irrationally knew belonged at the kitchen table.

Realizing what happened left Jake stunned. He tried again to lift himself from the chair but only raised it a few inches off the ground. The wheels of the leather office chair clattered as it settled back. He examined his restraints. Plastic zip ties secured his arms, and although he couldn't see, presumably the same thing held his feet tight against the cylinder holding the chair's gas lift.

Jake stared at the man sitting on the kitchen chair. He barely fit in the chair. His crinkly red hair looked matted, like he had been sweating profusely. He wore a wrinkled black hoodie over his barrel-shaped chest. He had no shoes—only grubby socks. Jake recalled the yellow running shoes catching his attention when Dani discovered Fletcher Patterson's body.

Jake said, "Lucas, right? Lucas Harmer? You're Cynthia's brother?"

The security guard grinned. "Good deduction, Jake. You don't mind if I call you Jake, do you?"

Jake stared at the man. The last name wasn't on the name tag Lucas wore when he let him and Dani into the building where Patterson was killed. He didn't know what Harmer had in store for him, but his best hope was to keep the man talking. He hoped the police officer had arrived and would check on him. His heart sank when he remembered asking Dani to tell the officer not to bother him because he planned to go to bed.

"You did a good job of pretending the sight of Fletcher Patterson's body sickened you, Lucas."

"I'm proud of that. I stuck my fingers down my throat to make myself throw up. Had to clean up my new runners after."

"Why did you torture Patterson? What did he do that caused that kind of treatment?"

"Oh, he did lots. I needed to understand whom he told what. He told me about you and how he planned to tell you everything. That part didn't bother me, except I wasn't sure which story he was going to tell you. There are two stories from 2009. The one everyone told and the actual story. He told me about the money laundering scheme, but I couldn't have cared less about that. He was the ringleader in 2009 when the incident happened. That's the real reason I tortured him."

"When *what* incident happened, and who is *everyone*? I know a lot less than you think I do."

"You talked to Professor Carpenter, but he doesn't know much. It's all speculation on his part. But now you've pieced things together, so… Something about a coded message, too."

Jake didn't know how much time had passed. It seemed like an eternity. He needed to keep Lucas talking as long as possible. He shook his head. "You're talking in riddles, and I don't have a clue what you're referring to. Why don't you tell me what happened in 2009? Let's start there."

Lucas hesitated and shuffled in his chair. He leaned back with his legs crossed at the ankles and his hands clasped across his belly. "Okay, you're not going to be around anyway, and it would be good to tell somebody. If I don't get out of this tonight, we're going to die together, Jake. I've accomplished what I needed to do, and I'm tired.

"It was the beginning of a new school year for all of us. Omar, Seda, Brenda, and Cynthia at the university in Ottawa and Craig and I in Kingston at the military college. Brenda changed her name to Francis, but I remember her as Brenda, so that's what I'll call her. Doesn't matter much now. She's dead. Craig and I spent the summer in Ottawa but planned to leave for university the next day. I didn't hang around with the group, but Craig invited me to a party they planned to mark the beginning of the new school year. Cynthia wasn't happy Craig invited me, but whatever. He did, and I went. It was a chilly night, but we found a spot by the river and sat around an open fire, drinking beer. Patterson provided drugs, which we all consumed. I don't know why no passersby saw the open fire. I wish they had.

"Cynthia told me Seda and Brenda always bullied her. My sister was socially awkward but an excellent student. She told me how Professor Carpenter gave her special treatment because she did so well in school. She hated the special attention he paid to her because the other students resented it, especially Seda and Brenda. They gave Cynthia a hard time about being a 'teacher's pet' at the party. Things got heated, and they started fighting. Cynthia, Brenda, and Seda. Obviously, Cynthia took the worst of it. We were already feeling the effects of the alcohol and drugs, so the guys laughed for a while, but eventually, we pulled them apart.

"The night carried on, and everybody got stoned out of their minds. Brenda and Seda whispered something to each other and then suggested Cynthia should race them to a buoy about 100 yards from shore. Cynthia was athletic and an excellent swimmer. When I thought about it after, she would've swum to the buoy and back no problem if she'd been sober, but the other two could never do it, sober or not. We all saw but not that well. Even with my judgment impaired, I realized that. I begged Cynthia not to go, but she insisted. The other guys yelled, 'Swim, swim, swim.' Cynthia caved to the peer pressure. She wanted to fit in. The girls stripped down to their underwear and jumped in the water. Everybody laughed when they dove in.

"Omar, Craig, and I sat around the fire talking. I remember hearing splashing, and then everything got eerily quiet. Brenda and Seda walked up like nothing happened. I asked where Cynthia was, and they said they didn't know."

Jake worked at his restraints as Lucas talked, but the zip ties showed no sign of loosening.

"I was frantic. I called out to Cynthia but with no answer. I waded into the water, but I'm not a skilled swimmer. I asked the group to help me, but they just talked among themselves. I couldn't hear what they were saying, so I grabbed my phone to call 911. Craig ripped the phone from my hands and threw it in the water. He pulled me aside and told me they had agreed they would say nothing to anyone, ever. He told me if I said anything to the police, they would say it was me who encouraged Cynthia to go into the water and that I did nothing to save her. Omar was dating Seda, and Craig was dating Brenda, so they were all in. They said they would make sure the police charged me with contributing to her death. I said nothing to the police. I already had a record for distributing drugs, so I just told the police the party line. That she must have gone for a swim after the party broke up. The dog walker found her the next day. I let my sister down. It devastated my parents, but I vowed to get even for them."

Jake interrupted Lucas's story. "Why didn't Patterson recognize you? You worked in the same building. He walked by you every day. You're recognizable with your size and red hair."

"That's the thing. He didn't recognize me until I told him who I was before I killed him. Sure, I've gained weight and grown my hair longer. I thought about it a lot. The night of the party, I wore a toque and had let my beard grow. It was dark that night, and Patterson barely paid attention to me. I found out where he worked, and when I saw the ad in the paper for the job, I jumped at the opportunity. I wanted him to see me every day as a reminder, but he never looked at me. Not once. He'd walk by in the morning and at night with his nose in the air. It was like I didn't exist for him. I worked in that building for two weeks, and he never looked at me once. Not once! If he did glance at me, he never actually *saw* me. That made me want revenge even more. You can believe I made him look at me before I stuck the knife in him.

"I waited fifteen years. Fifteen years! I wanted everyone together when I took my revenge, and I almost gave up. I thought it would never happen. Then, Craig decided to organize a reunion. I couldn't believe it! I don't know if they planned to toast staying out of prison or what. Craig even had the nerve to invite me. I guess he thought I'd let bygones be bygones. Instead, I hired a guy, an electrician I met during my time in the military. We tapped Omar's phone, and I found out the Demirs just had an electric stove installed, so the guy used that excuse to get in the house. He needed the money desperately. Kind of down on his luck, you know? Gambling debts or something. I told him to open the gas valve, and static electricity, or a spark of some kind, would do the rest. I told him he wouldn't be responsible for killing them since all he did was turn the valve, and he accepted that. Just my luck, Patterson walked away before the explosion happened."

"The electrician you're talking about is Warren Belton?"

"That's the guy. He didn't ask questions, but he became a liability when you put things together, so he had to go. I told him to watch you and be obvious about it, hoping it would scare you off. But you kept digging. I give you credit for persistence. With that kind of persistence, maybe if you'd been around to investigate when Cynthia died, things would've been different."

Jake didn't think so. His colleague, Janice, didn't discover the truth about the coverup, so he doubted he would have either.

"Did you know there was another person at the Bed and Breakfast? A young lady named Willow Altman. What about her?"

"I read about her. Collateral damage. I'm sorry about her."

Jake's head pulsated nonstop. "Did you know she was pregnant, Lucas? She wasn't much younger than your sister. How can you justify killing her? She had her whole life ahead of her." Jake's voice rose with every word.

"Settle down, Jake, or we'll end this right now. I feel bad she died, but she wasn't my sister."

"I have another question, Lucas. How did you know I talked to Professor Carpenter? You said you tapped Omar's phone. Did you do the same to me?"

"I've been listening to your calls for a while. You and the detective get along well. Too bad about your daughter. I hope she recovers. Yeah, we tapped your phone the same way as Omar's. It's easy when you know what you're doing. Do you remember a text message from UPS saying they couldn't deliver a package to you because they didn't have your correct address? You clicked on the link, and that installed a virus on your phone called a Remote Access Terminal, a RAT. I had access to your phone after that. Something else I learned in the military. The military was good for something."

Jake felt stupid for falling for the scam, but he said, "Why didn't you just go to the police, Lucas? Why don't you call them now? I can help you tell your story."

"I couldn't go at the time because it was my word against five. Don't you see? I had a record for drug offenses. I would have been in jail for years for involuntary manslaughter. The police would have made the case I was criminally negligent by not helping. I just took care of it myself, and I'm at peace now they're all dead."

"What about the marks on Cynthia from the beating she took? You could've explained that to the police. That would've helped your case."

"They were all going to say I did that. Make up some story about how Cynthia and I got into a fight. And now I've killed Patterson and Belton, there's no hope. I've done what I set out to do. I've got my revenge. It's too late for the police, Jake. You seem like a smart guy. Persistent. A good guy. But I need to tidy up loose ends. Maybe I can get out of this yet, but I can't leave you behind after everything I've told you. I assume you have a gas stove?"

CHAPTER FIFTY-ONE

JAKE CALLED OUT to Lucas as he strode from the room. "Don't do this, Lucas. You're just making it worse for yourself." He yanked on the restraints but just cut and bruised his wrists and ankles. Something dripped inside the neck of his shirt. *It must be blood from the wound where Lucas hit me.* No wonder his head pulsed in and out like an accordion.

Jake desperately scanned the office for something sharp. He remembered the letter opener in the desk — if he could somehow reach it and nudge the drawer open. He dug his toes into the carpet and pushed. The chair moved forward about six inches. He tried again and again. Each time the chair moved a few inches, but a distance remained between him and the desk. He thought he heard a hissing sound coming from the kitchen area. Maybe it was his imagination, or did Lucas actually turn on the gas?

Lucas's enormous frame loomed in the doorway to the office, accompanied by a sulfuric, rotten egg odor. He hauled Jake's chair back to the center of the office. "What's in the desk? Must be something sharp. Nice try, but here's how it's going to work, Jake. The gas buildup won't take long. I noticed your new windows, so your house is nice and airtight. Soon, the house will fill with gas. At first, you'll be tired, maybe nauseous and dizzy. You might even feel happy for a few minutes. Then, some chest pain for a bit. You'll eventually pass out, and that'll be it. Or, if your police friends come to the door and turn on the light switch, Ka-boom!"

Jake stared at Lucas. He had nothing to say. He desperately tried to think of a way out of this, but nothing came to mind. His heart sank as his thoughts turned to Avery, wondering how she was doing and if he would ever see his grandchild. He thought of Dani, wishing he had told her how much he cared for her. As Lucas predicted, fatigue muddled his brain, and bile crept up his throat. Emilie came to his mind, and he realized how much he cared for the teenager. He wanted to watch her grow up. He tried to picture her, but his head drifted toward his chest. It took all his strength to will his neck to straighten.

The odor became stronger. Jake wretched. The walls seemed to shimmy as if he were wandering in the desert sun. *Where am I?* His eyes wanted to close, but he forced them open. A framed picture on the wall seemed to tilt. Something landed on his lap. *What now?* His mind urged him just to inhale deeply. He wanted to give up. Fall asleep, never to wake again. *Get this over with.* The thing on his lap moved and rubbed against his chest. Jake hadn't realized his eyes had closed. His hands and feet were still bound to the chair, but even if they hadn't been, he wasn't sure he could move. *So tired.* He pried his eyes open to see a shimmering image of Lucas staring at him from the doorway. It was as if a fog enveloped him as Lucas's image faded in and out.

Jake heard a familiar purring sound. His head wobbled as he cast his eyes down to see a distorted image of Oliver nestling on his lap. His foggy mind was happy to see the cat, who wretched from the gas like he had a fur ball. Jake thought he would die with Oliver sitting on his lap. Kind of fitting. *Wait!* Something tickled at his addled brain. Something wasn't right. A thought coalesced. *Oliver was outside, wasn't he?* Jake tried to force himself to concentrate. *Who let him in?*

He still felt disoriented and nauseous but more aware than before. Seeing the cat somehow breathed life into his drained body. The sign of life renewed his hope that, somehow, he would get out of this. His sight cleared enough that when he glanced at the doorway, he saw realization dawning on Lucas. He, too, focused on Oliver. Widening eyes above the handkerchief Lucas held over his mouth gave Jake some satisfaction. Lucas's eyes darted from the cat to the patio door. Jake sensed a whiff of fresh air drifting into the office. As the life-giving air reached his nostrils, Jake's mind cleared a little, and he understood that someone opened the patio door. *That's where Oliver came from!*

The sound of Dani's shouting voice echoed through Jake's addled brain.

"STOP RIGHT THERE, LUCAS."

Dani remained out of sight from Jake's angle, but he imagined her advancing with her gun in a two-handed grip.

Lucas pulled an electric lighter from his pocket. "I wouldn't come any closer, Detective. Smart to open the door, but there's still enough gas in here to blow us all to smithereens."

"Put the lighter down, Lucas. What good are you doing now? Everyone's dead that had anything to do with your sister's death. You're not accomplishing anything now. Drop the lighter."

Jake's chest hurt, and his eyes still wouldn't focus, but the fresh air displacing the gas through the patio door cleared his brain. It slowly dawned on him that Dani couldn't shoot until more of the gas cleared. The discharge would set off an explosion. Everyone must know that. Dani. Lucas. *Did Lucas care at this point?* Jake stared helplessly, watching a scene unfold he could not control.

Or could he?

Lucas thumbed the button on the electric lighter, ready to ignite the flame. A press of the button and they would all be dead. Torn apart by the ensuing explosion. "I suggest you leave the house, Detective. I don't care anymore if I die tonight. My job is done. Like you said, everyone responsible for my sister's death is gone. Three of us will die if you stick around much longer."

Jake dug his toes into the carpet and pushed his butt forward at the same time, propelling the chair with all his remaining strength. He wondered if the chair's castors would generate static electricity on the floor to ignite the gas. It didn't before when he pushed toward the desk, but, oh, yes, that was before the gas buildup. He had to try. Jake willed Dani to keep Lucas distracted as his chair edged closer. Oliver shifted on his lap but seemed content to stay curled up.

Lucas's complete attention rested on Dani. "I'll give you to the count of ten to leave. I'll give you another ten to clear everyone out of the area. Then, the entire house goes up. Understand?"

Jake heard Dani's muffled voice, "Tell everyone to move back," followed by mumbled voices Jake couldn't understand. Dani added in a much louder tone, "I said move everyone back. Now!"

Jake continued to inch his chair forward until about three feet remained between him and Lucas. Fortunately, Lucas still stared in Dani's direction. Oliver was fully awake now and preparing to leap off Jake's lap. Jake's heart pounded. He swallowed hard twice to keep the contents of his stomach in place. The sulfuric odor still hung in the air and on his tongue. He inched his chair forward.

Lucas started his countdown. Sweat poured in rivulets down his cheek and the back of his neck. He trembled as his thumb closed on the lighter's button.

… 6-5-4…

Jake inched forward.

Dani was visible beyond Lucas through the doorway now. She stood as he imagined. Her gun pointed unwavering at Lucas's chest. Her face a mask of grim determination. Jake thought he saw her eyes shift towards him ever so slightly.

Lucas did, too. He sped up his count as he glanced at Jake, who now sat right behind him. Lucas's thumb tightened on the lighter's button.

Jake's chair moved another couple of inches.

… 3-2…

Jake launched himself and the chair at Lucas. It wasn't the power move he imagined. His legs buckled, weakened by his ordeal, but he pressed his toes into the floor enough to gain leverage and pitched himself and the chair forward. Oliver bailed out and hightailed for the patio door as Jake made his move. Jake and the chair became one awkward projectile, and he would have landed on his face if Lucas hadn't been there. The top of the chair caught Lucas at waist level, smashing him toward the wall. Jake couldn't tell what was going on, but Lucas lost his balance and toppled over with a thud. Jake landed face down, pressed against Lucas's back with the chair on top of him. Lucas struggled, pinned against the floor and wall by the combined weight of Jake's body and the chair.

Jake had no idea where the lighter went, but he hoped it landed out of Lucas's reach. Chaos erupted as Dani shouted instructions. "Get in here! Open the doors and windows. Don't turn on any lights. I repeat, DO NOT TURN ON ANY LIGHTS. Do nothing that might create a spark." Jake heard her kick an object, which he assumed to be the lighter, as it helicoptered across the floor. "Lucas Harmer," she continued, "you're under arrest for the murder of Omar Demir, Seda Demir, also known as Seda Aydin, Craig Thorpe, Francis Thorpe, also known as Brenda Rutledge, Fletcher Patterson, Willow Altman and her unborn child, and Warren Belton. Also, for the attempted murder of Jake Scott."

She continued reading Lucas his rights as she shoved Jake and the chair sideways off him. She produced a knife and cut Jake's plastic ties while pointing at Lucas and yelling at a constable, "Cuff him and get him out of here."

For the first time, Jake saw Dani's bare feet, cotton tee shirt, and jeans. "Nice outfit," he joked feebly as Dani draped a blanket over his shoulders and led him down the hall to the door at the front of the house.

"Yeah, well, the last thing we needed was a static electricity spark from my clothes."

CHAPTER FIFTY-TWO

JAKE SPENT A few hours in the hospital for observation, but the doctor soon determined someone in worse shape needed the bed and sent him home. The doctor credited Dani for forcing Jake to drink two bottles of water immediately after leaving the gas-filled house and prescribed more liquids, rest, and lots of fresh air for a full recovery. Jake left the hospital completely unhappy about the white bandage encircling his head to cover the stitches in the wound Lucas gave him. He didn't relish the attention the bandage would draw.

The fire department cleared Jake's house during the night. Fortunately, open windows and doors and a light north breeze removed all remnants of natural gas. Dani had to drop into work to file her report. The neighbors gossiped nonstop about the night's commotion the next morning.

When Jake arrived home, scrapes on the wall in front of the door to the office told the story of what transpired during the night. The walls would require a touch of joint compound, sanding, and a paint job. Jake planned to hire a professional to fix that. His clumsy launch of the chair like a slow-moving missile bent the wheels, and a large tear in the seat spilled foam material. Otherwise, no one would ever know something chilling occurred during the night.

Worried about Avery, Jake called Nick before tumbling into bed. Nick confirmed Avery was still resting in intensive care. He assured Jake he would call first thing in the morning. Jake fell into bed and, despite his apprehension about Avery, slept the sleep of the dead.

Jake showered and dressed in blue shorts and a white short-sleeve shirt. He enjoyed eggs and toast for breakfast, let Oliver into the backyard, and pulled a lawn chair away from the patio table. The large, brown umbrella rose with a few cranks of the handle, and he slid a matching chair into the shade. He pulled his sunglasses from his chest pocket, put them on, and took a deep breath to fill his lungs with the refreshing fresh air prescribed by the doctor. Wispy shape-shifting clouds meandered across the cerulean sky. He leaned back in his chair, observing them with a bottle of chilled water in his hand. Oliver returned from wherever he was and curled up in the shade beside Jake. He hadn't left Jake's side, other than to do his business and for this brief foray to investigate the back of the yard, since the previous night's events.

Jake hadn't heard from Nick, so he leaned forward with his elbows on his knees and dialed his number. Nick answered immediately.

"I was just about to call you with good news, Jake. Avery is out of intensive care and in a regular bed. She's awake, talking, and laughing. She's in great spirits. The doctors say she'll make a full recovery, and the baby will be fine, too. They've cleared her to go home soon. She's in the bathroom now, but we can call you back in a few minutes."

Jake let out a long breath as the immense weight lifted from his shoulders. He imagined it floating upward to join the clouds in the sky. "I can't tell you how happy I am, Nick. That's such great news. I was worried sick. Give her my love and a big hug from Oliver and me. Dani sends her love, too. She's coming over soon, and we're going for lunch at Brew and Buns, so we'll call back when we return if that's okay."

Nick laughed. "I love that name. Anyway, did you solve the case of the mysterious message?"

"As a matter of fact, we did. Dani did all the heavy lifting as she usually does. The perpetrator is behind bars now where he should be, and everyone is safe. I'm sure the courts will hold him responsible for a lot of deaths." Jake decided not to elaborate. He would explain everything to Avery and Nick when they got together. Perhaps. Sometimes, the less his daughter knew about his escapades, the better, especially after going through her own trauma.

The squeak of tires on hot pavement drifted around the corner from the front of the house as Jake hung up. The tires chirped to a stop in front of the garage. Jake smiled, imagining his speed demon girlfriend executing the turn and coming to a stop a few inches from the garage door, all while in complete control of a 4,000-pound vehicle. She sauntered around the corner into the backyard wearing a blue V-neck top with khaki shorts and white running shoes. Her hair was tied back in a ponytail that stuck through the opening at the back of a Blue Jays baseball hat.

She gave Jake a peck on the cheek. "How're you feeling now?" she asked.

"I'm great. Are you hungry?"

"That bandage makes you look like you just returned from a war. I guess, in a way, you did. Just a sec. I need a picture." Despite Jake's protests, she snapped the picture and set her phone on the table. Dani said, "I'm famished. I've been looking forward to this all morning. You must promise not to throw any chairs at anyone. Especially if you're sitting in them." She chuckled. "That maneuver you made with the chair is so fresh in my mind. It wasn't pretty, but it sure was effective. Lucas didn't see that coming. I'm not sure how you accomplished the maneuver tied up like that. Fortunately, he didn't touch the button on the lighter before you hit him. They would have been scraping us up in Toronto."

Jake grinned as he rose from his chair to let Oliver into the house. "I don't want to consider how close we came. I'll meet you at the front, and we'll wander over to Brew and Buns." He hurried inside to close the windows and lock the patio door. He even set the security alarm on the way out the front door, which he decided would become a more frequent occurrence.

As they wandered hand-in-hand down the street to the restaurant, Jake told Dani the good news about Avery. Her face lit in a broad smile. She said, "I'm so happy to hear that. You must be relieved."

Jake couldn't agree more as they arrived at the restaurant and sat at a table on the outdoor patio. "Too nice to go inside," Dani said.

They ordered a pitcher of beer from Amanda, beer-battered fish and chips for him, and a salmon wrap for her.

Jake said, "So, how did you know Lucas was in the house with me?"

"I wondered when you would ask that. After I talked to you last night, Forensics told me they identified a smudged fingerprint on a cigarette butt one of my detectives found behind the toilet in the bathroom where Patterson was killed. Can you imagine? On a cigarette butt. Forensics never cease to amaze me, and they're getting better all the time. They're magicians. Lucas may have tried to toss the cigarette in the toilet after torturing Patterson and missed. Enough detail remained on the cigarette that they matched the fingerprint to Lucas. He was in the system, thanks to his drug conviction.

"We were going to pick him up for questioning. I called the constable assigned to your house to make sure everything was okay, and he said he saw lights at the back of your house. He said you turned out the kitchen light and looked out the window, but I was worried about you. You told me how exhausted you were and said you were going to bed right away. I had to check on you. I tried the front door, which was locked, of course, but I had a feeling something was wrong, so I went around to the back patio door. It surprised me to find it unlocked."

Amanda brought their frosty beer pitcher along with two glasses and set them on the table. She stared and raised an eyebrow at Jake's bandaged head but seemed to decide not to ask.

Jake said, "Kitchen cabinet."

Amanda nodded with one eyebrow cocked and said she had no time to talk but asked how they were doing otherwise. They answered in unison, "Living the dream," and laughed. Jake poured each of them a glass of the amber liquid, and they toasted quietly to being alive, to Avery, Nick, and Jake's future grandchild. Amanda left to go about her duties.

"Your intuition is unbelievable, Dani. You should always listen to it. It's truly amazing. Oliver startled me when he landed on my lap. I was groggy, so it took me a few seconds to figure out what was going on and more time to remember I put him outside."

Dani sipped her beer, leaving white froth remaining around her lips, which she wiped with the back of her hand. "That cat was a potentially huge problem. He blended in with the dark of the backyard, and the second I slid the door open, he darted past me. The good news is that he led me to you. It could have been disastrous if the gas hadn't slowed Lucas's thought processes just like yours. I pulled my gun on Lucas before he realized what was happening."

Their food arrived as Jake thought about the gun. He set his napkin on his lap as he said, "You couldn't have pulled the trigger, right? That would've set off an explosion."

Dani bit into her salmon wrap and smiled as juice dribbled down her chin. Jake's heart melted at the sight of Dani's smile, even with the drop of juice about to fall onto her lap. She caught the drop with her napkin at the last second. As she finished dabbing at her chin, she said, "I tried to prolong the discussion long enough that the fresh air coming through the patio door would replace enough of the gas. The gas still smelled strong. Plan B was to rush him before he finished his countdown. You beat me to it."

"You said it was lucky you dressed the way you did so you wouldn't set off a spark. But it was bare feet, jeans, and a tee shirt. How did you know you wore the right clothes?"

Dani laughed. "From paying attention when I do laundry, Jake. All my clothes last night were cotton, which doesn't create static. I happened to wear cotton. I didn't plan to walk into a house filled with gas."

They continued enjoying their meals in silence, each lost in what could have been. Jake decided to forget about that somehow and concentrate on what would be.

CHAPTER FIFTY-THREE

JAKE AND DANI finished their meals and wandered back down the street. Dani scrolled through her phone on the way to the house and said, "Do you know what tomorrow is?"

Jake sifted through possibilities in his mind like flipping through a paper calendar. He wondered if it was some date he should remember, like their first official date or first kiss or something, but he came up with nothing.

When he admitted it, Dani said, "Saturday, and the group is gathering for breakfast at Brew and Buns. Should we go? We'll get lots of questions since Lucas's arrest appeared in this morning's paper, and they'll publish more tomorrow, too. And then there's that whopping big bandage on your head."

"It won't matter if we go this week or wait 'til next week. They'll always have questions. I'll make up some story about the bandage. Sure, let's go."

Jake called Avery and put the phone on speaker so he and Dani could both converse with her. They spoke for about ten minutes. Although in good spirits, she sounded exhausted. Jake told her they planned to drive to Toronto to visit in two days and stay in a hotel. Avery acknowledged sleepily how thrilled she was that they were coming.

Jake and Dani spent the afternoon enjoying each other's company, and Jake barbecued burgers for supper. An eerie sensation overcame him when he turned on the natural gas to light the barbecue, especially when a whiff drifted up from the grill. It would take a while to forget that smell.

Dani praised Jake on his barbecuing skills as they enjoyed wine with their meal. He sat pensively after supper.

"What's bothering you, Jake? You're awfully quiet."

"I was just thinking about the people at the Bed and Breakfast. They all kept secrets hidden. You just never know what is going on in people's lives, do you?"

"No, you don't, Jake. I've learned that the hard way in my job."

"What will happen with the rug scheme, or should I say money laundering scheme?"

"The Fraud Unit is still investigating, but the local arm of the scheme is shut down, obviously, since all the principals are dead. The Demirs and Patterson are gone. They used Patterson as a pawn. Based on the message he left, I suspect he planned to tell you about Cynthia Harmer.

"The Demirs were lower-level players facilitating money laundering. The RCMP will investigate other Turkish rug stores in the country that may front for money laundering to try to find the top-level players. It's an enormous task. Of course, Seda and Brenda might have been convicted of Cynthia's murder if Lucas had spoken up years ago, but who knows? If they all stuck to their story, even if Lucas finally came forward, the case would've been five against one. Lucas was right. Not very good odds for him."

Jake nodded. "What about Craig and Francis Thorpe? Brenda Rutledge. Whatever we want to call her. Quite a tale those two ended up telling with their death."

"Hard to say what would have happened to them if they had lived, Jake. They would have potentially gone to jail for Cynthia's murder, of course, but maybe they both would have received the treatment they needed in prison. Clearly, Craig needed more help for his PTSD, and Francis seemed to need help period. My investigators are looking into the threatening letters Francis received, but they were most likely from the family of the person who died when she pretended to be a nurse."

Jake said, "I remember Craig's mother saying he met Francis somewhere. I guess she didn't know where exactly."

"No, I guess she didn't," Dani replied.

The sun drifted behind neighboring houses, and a chill filled the air. Dani wrapped her arms around herself until she noticed Jake staring at the table and tugging at his bottom lip.

Dani reached for his hand. "Now Willow's on your mind, right?"

"Yeah, she was an innocent bystander. She made mistakes, but she sure didn't deserve to die. And her baby, too. I think of Avery and Nick and how scared all of us, including you, were when she had her problems. Willow's death must've devastated her poor family."

"Yes, our team is following up on that, too. Dan Rivera is going to be charged with assault, and the baby's father came forward. He seems like a decent enough person. He wants to pay Willow's funeral expenses to help the family. I didn't tell you because we were kind of busy. Aren't you cold? It's freezing out here."

Jake came out of his stupor with a grin. He didn't think it was *that* cold. In fact, the evening had turned rather pleasant, but Jake wasn't a stupid man.

"Let's go inside," he said as he rose from his chair.

CHAPTER FIFTY-FOUR

DANI SPENT THE night with Jake and was delighted to see when she checked her phone in the morning that no murders occurred in Ottawa overnight. It wasn't like Ottawa was the murder capital, but she thought it would be her luck if there was another one. The stabbing case in the Byward Market had been wrapped up. She reveled in taking time off as she accompanied Jake down the street to Brew and Buns. Yesterday's gorgeous weather carried forward to the morning. Abundant sunshine. Little wind. No humidity. No bugs. Idyllic.

She said as they neared the restaurant, "I wonder what the big subject will be this week. My guess is sports, electric cars, and travel, and we may touch on more sports. Oh, and your bandage, of course."

"That sounds about right, Dani. All I know is I have a great word to throw into the conversation with Pierre when I get the opportunity. It was Alexa's word of the day. I heard it when you were in the shower. The word is 'buccula.'"

"I know you've been doing this for months, Jake. It's the little game you play to get back at Pierre for being the meany he can be sometimes. Okay, I'll bite. What on earth does buccula mean?"

"The official definition is a 'fatty puffing under the chin,' but the more common definition is 'double chin.'"

Dani examined Jake's chin. "Are you sure you want to go there?" she teased.

Jake looked aghast. "Are you saying *I* have a double chin?"

Dani laughed and said, "Yes, but yours is adorable."

They agreed that it would be nice to sit on the patio but acknowledged the group would never want to relinquish the chairs they sat in every week.

They arrived at the restaurant and found their usual group gathered around the round table in the same seats they sat in since the gathering began, like knights entrusted with the quest to find the Holy Grail. The two chairs left vacant between Eric Jacobson and Pierre Chevrier waited for Jake and Dani to complete the circle.

The three men glanced at Jake. Pierre beat the others to it when he said, "Whoa, what happened to you?"

Jake grinned and suggested he left a cabinet door open in his office and knocked himself silly when he stood up. No one bought the explanation based on the skeptical faces around the table. He touched the bandage self-consciously. The wound itched like crazy.

Dani and Jake slid the chairs back to sit down.

Amanda arrived right behind them with coffee as Jake told his story about whacking his head. As she poured, Amanda played along. She said, "I wondered what happened yesterday and was going to ask, but the bandage looked fresh, so I thought I'd give you a chance to make up an excuse." Bending to Jake's ear level, she whispered, "You told me it was a kitchen cabinet." She stood and winked at Jake as her notepad appeared with a flourish, ready to take their orders. She put the notepad away again when everyone ordered the same things they always did.

Eric said, "So Dani, I see you caught the person who caused the big explosion that almost killed our friend Jake here." He slapped Jake on the back. "It sounds like a long, interesting story. Care to elaborate for us?"

The three men leaned forward in anticipation as Dani sipped her coffee. "It wasn't all me, but yes, we caught him. We should eat first. I'm famished. Anyway, in more interesting news, Jake's going to be a grandpa. Right, Jake?"

Jake glanced at Dani, thinking he owed her one for deflecting the conversation to him. Eric, Pierre, and Ryan congratulated him with enough volume everyone in the room turned their heads. The three men peppered him with questions about when the baby would be born, whether it would be a boy or girl, and so on. They appeared genuinely interested, and Jake proudly gave them as much information as he could without divulging Avery's recent stay in the hospital.

As their meals arrived, Dani's guess on the topics of the day proved accurate. She would later say she didn't have to be a rocket scientist to guess the topics when she sat with a table full of guys.

Pierre pointed his fork at Jake's eggs with crispy bacon. He slurred through a mouthful of egg, "Are you off your diet again, Jake?"

Jake examined a piece of crispy bacon stuck between the tines of his fork. "Yup, I can't wait to add to my buccula."

He smiled at Dani, who pursed her lips, her eyes bulging. It took her a few seconds to swallow her orange juice. Pierre sat in stunned silence while Eric and Ryan smiled in confused understanding. They didn't understand the word, but they understood why Jake used it.

They continued their conversation and gathered outside in a circle after paying their bills. Five friends who had been meeting together for years. Jake said, "Dani and I won't be here next Saturday. We're going to Toronto to be with Avery and Nick for a few days."

"Okay, safe travels, you two," Ryan said.

Eric said, "Have a great time."

Pierre said, "Stay out of trouble," with a smirk.

Jake smiled, deciding all was right with the world as he and Dani went their separate ways to pack.

Thank you for reading *The Secret Truth*. If you like what you read, please consider leaving a review at your favorite online book retailer.

QUESTIONS TO START YOUR BOOK CLUB DISCUSSION

1. Describe the personalities and motivations of the main characters in *The Secret Truth*. Did you find them to be fully developed?
2. At what point in the book did you begin to figure out whether the explosion was accidental or deliberate?
3. Did you identify any hidden clues?
4. Did the author try to throw you off track and if so, how?
5. Did the twists and turns enhance the story and add to the suspense?
6. At what point did the suspense start to build?
7. Is the conclusion probable and believable?
8. Were there any questions left unresolved in the story?
9. Overall, did the book satisfy you? Is there anything you would see happening differently?
10. Have you read the other books in the *Jake Scott Mystery Series*? How does *The Secret Truth* compare?

ABOUT THE AUTHOR

Barry Finlay is the award-winning author of the travel adventure, *Kilimanjaro and Beyond – A Life-Changing Journey* (with his son Chris), the Amazon bestselling travel memoir, *I Guess We Missed The Boat*, the inspirational *Just Keep Climbing*, and five Amazon bestselling and award-winning thrillers comprising The Marcie Kane Thriller Collection: *The Vanishing Wife, A Perilous Question, Remote Access, Never So Alone*, and *The Burden of Darkness*. His new Jake Scott Mystery Series debuted with *Searching For Truth* and *The Guardians of Truth*. He is now following that up with *The Secret Truth*. Barry was featured in the 2012-13 Authors Show's edition of "50 Great Writers You Should Be Reading." He is a recipient of the Queen Elizabeth Diamond Jubilee medal for his fundraising efforts to help kids in Tanzania, Africa. Barry lives with his wife Evelyn in Ottawa, Canada.

Contact Barry Finlay

Author Website: **www.barry-finlay.com**

BOOKS BY BARRY FINLAY

THE JAKE SCOTT MYSTERY SERIES

Searching For Truth: A Jake Scott Mystery (Book 1)
The Guardians of Truth: A Jake Scott Mystery (Book 2)
The Secret Truth: A Jake Scott Mystery (Book 3)

THE MARCIE KANE THRILLER COLLECTION

The Vanishing Wife: An Action-Packed Crime Thriller (Marcie Kane Book 1)
A Perilous Question: An International Thriller & Crime Novel (Marcie Kane Book 2)
Remote Access: An International Political Thriller (Marcie Kane Book 3)
Never So Alone (Prequel novella to the Marcie Kane Thriller Collection)—Book 4)
The Burden of Darkness: A Marcie Kane and Nathan Harris Thriller (Marcie Kane Book 5)

NON-FICTION TITLES

Kilimanjaro and Beyond: A Life-Changing Journey
I Guess We Missed the Boat
Just Keep Climbing: Inspirational Stories for Overcoming Challenges and Living Life

FIND THEM ONLINE OR AT YOUR FAVORITE BOOK STORE OR LIBRARY

READ THE FIRST TWO BOOKS IN THE EXCITING JAKE SCOTT MYSTERY SERIES

SEARCHING FOR TRUTH

Former journalist Jake Scott relies on his weekly breakfast gatherings with friends and a temperamental tabby cat named Oliver to keep his spirits up. He has lost his wife, retired from his job, and watched his daughter move to Toronto with her boyfriend.

Things change when one of the breakfast attendees, a beautiful and tenacious police detective with a troubled teenage daughter, suggests Jake should write a book. When he takes her advice and researches a convicted murderer's case, he finds out something is terribly wrong. Could a member of the breakfast group be hiding a secret deadly enough to commit murder?

Jake follows leads that uncover a mysterious and disturbing rollercoaster ride of clues, all while his attraction for the detective grows. An attempt to force the true murderer out of hiding results in a terrifying ordeal on the coldest night of the year.

GUARDIANS OF TRUTH

The affable and shrewd, yet old-fashioned, Jake is hot on the trail of a case when a body discovered in a bog and three suspects lead him to the doorstep of The Guardians of Truth, a shady organization with an opportunistic and charismatic leader. While the organization purports to offer everlasting support to its followers, Jake discovers just the opposite is true. Now Jake and an insider, Cassie Wright, want to expose the leader and protect his followers from financial ruin or worse. Their harrowing quest isn't without peril, as one will disappear and the other will be forced to fight for survival.

If you like your heroes to be, well, like you and me, the second book in the Jake Scott Mystery Series will draw you in and have you wishing you could dive in to help.

www.barry-finlay.com